英 語 で 紹 介 す る

寿司

ハンドブック

A SUSHI HANDBOOK
IN ENGLISH AND JAPANESE

銀座 久兵衛

今田洋輔

［監修］

ナツメ社

はじめに

　気が付いたら50年、18歳でこの世界に入り、記念すべき年に本書を出すこととなりました。今までやってきた仕事の集大成とも言えます。

　寿司は鮮度の高い**素材**と適切に炊かれた**シャリ**、腕の良い**板前**の3つで成り立つ料理です。素材のうまさを引き出し、楽しむことが料理と言うなれば、寿司はその核に一番近い所にある

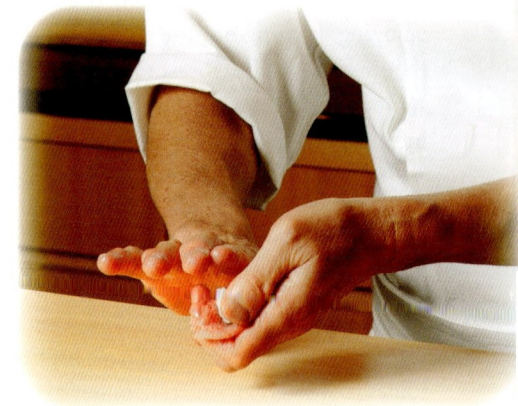

のではないでしょうか。

　なぜ寿司が国際的にも日本を代表する料理になり得たのか？ それは旨かったからに他なりません！ 他にも複合的な理由がありますが、旨くなくては広がりません。

　では海外の寿司とどこが違うのか？ まず素材の質（日本は地形的に恵まれている）、漁師の技術（一匹一匹手釣りで生きた魚が手に入る）、迅速な流通経路と魚を傷めない丁寧なケア。そして、魚の命を頂く我々の技術。そのネタの命を損なうことなく、生かし切るのが板前の使命なのです。

　将来、ネタも変わっていくでしょう。それに即応できる柔軟な頭と技術が必要となります。手を掛けすぎて寿司本来の旨さを損なわないよう、願っています。

　本書を上梓させて頂き、皆様の知識と寿司観が変わることができれば、望外の喜びでございます。

銀座 久兵衛　今田洋輔

Preface

I entered the world of sushi when I was eighteen years old, and before I knew it, fifty years had already passed. This book will be published in a commemorative year for me and it could be said to be an compilation of my life's work thus far.

Sushi is a cuisine that requires three elements: extremely fresh ingredients; *shari* (sushi rice) that has been cooked just right; and a good sushi chef. If cooking can be defined as enjoying drawing out the delicious flavor of the ingredients, then sushi must be closest to the very heart of cooking.

How did sushi come to be representative of Japan's cuisine internationally? That must be because it is so delicious! There are many other reasons but if sushi was not so tasty, then it would not have become so widespread.

How is sushi in Japan different to sushi abroad? Firstly, the quality of the ingredients (Japan is blessed from a geographical perspective); the techniques of fishermen (fish are caught one at a time enabling procurement of fresh fish); and prompt distribution routes as well as extreme care to not damage the fish. Along with these elements, the techniques of sushi chefs, who prepare the fish while giving thanks for nature's precious bounty, should be included. A sushi chef's mission is to make the most out of the fish.

In future, sushi toppings will most likely change. What is needed on the part of the sushi chef will be a flexible attitude and techniques to adapt quickly. I hope that the true delicious taste of sushi will not be spoilt by too much fiddling around with the ingredients.

In bringing out this book, I shall be extremely happy if about the way you think about sushi changes and you can increase your knowledge about this delicious food.

Ginza Kyubey Yosuke Imada

目次 CONTENTS

◆ 光り物　　*HIKARIMONO* Silver-skinned fish　57

◆ イカ・タコ　　*IKA/TAKO* Squid/Octopus　75

[第3章] 寿司をより深く知るために   141

Chapter 3 : Getting to know sushi more deeply

魚の名前

（漢字・平仮名・ローマ字・英語）
寿司屋で注文するときにこの通り言えば
通じる。

Fish names (Chinese charac-
ters/Hiragana (Japanese alphabet)/
Romanization/English)

The chefs at the sushi restaurant
will understand your order if you pro-
nounce the fish name like this.

寿司の写真

左ページで紹介している寿司ネタの写真。
※寿司の写真は「銀座 久兵衛」で握ら
れたもの。

Sushi photographs

Photographs of the sushi ingredients featured on the left hand page.
※ The sushi photographs were tak-
en at the Ginza Kyubey restaurant.

旬の季節

魚の旬の時期を季節
とカレンダーで紹介。

Best of
the seasons

The best times for
eating each fish,
introduced season
by season with a
calendar.

解説

それぞれの寿司ネタの産地
や旬の時期、味わいなどを
詳しく解説。江戸前寿司な
らではの調理法なども紹介
している。

Explanations

Detailed explanations
are provided of where
the sushi ingredients are
harvested, the best time
of year to eat them, how
they taste, methods of
preparation unique to
Edomae-zushi and more.

魚のデータ

寿司ネタになっている魚
の詳しいデータ。主産地
や地方での呼び方、世
界での分布域が分かる。

Fish facts

Detailed data on the
fish used as sushi in-
gredients, telling you
about their main har-
vesting areas, local
names for the fish,
and their distribution
throughout the world.

寿司を食べる前に知っておきたい3つのこと

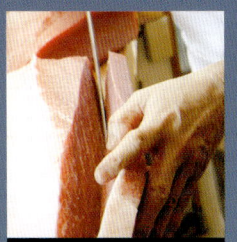

Chapter **1**

Three things
you should know
before eating sushi

① 寿司とは？ What is sushi?

　寿司は、酢飯（→P.84）と主に魚介類を組み合わせた日本の伝統的な料理である。鮨、鮓とも書く。寿司は生鮮の魚介に酢を使った「早寿司」と、魚介に米を加えて発酵させた「熟れ寿司」に大別される。いわゆる「SUSHI」は、早寿司のなかでも代表的な江戸前の「握り寿司」を指す。

　握り寿司は、魚介などのネタの上に山葵（→P.94）をつけ、一口大のシャリ（寿司飯、酢飯）をのせて握ったもの。誕生したのは江戸時代後期で、当時は屋台で立ったまま食べる手軽なファストフードであった。

　今日、健康食志向からも、寿司人気は高まり、日本はもとより、海外でも一定の地位を獲得したといってよいだろう。

Sushi is a traditional type of Japanese cuisine composed mainly of a combination of *sumeshi* (vinegared rice),[1] fish or shellfish. The most commonly used Japanese character for sushi is "寿司" but is the first character is also sometimes written "鮨" or "鮓". Sushi can be broadly divided into *hayazushi*, where the vinegar is used with fish, and *narezushi*, in which the fish is fermented together with rice.Usually, sushi refers to the representative type of hayazushi, namely *edomae nigiri-zushi*.

In *nigiri-zushi*, wasabi (Japanese horseradish)[2] is dabbed onto the fish or shellfish, and placed on top of an oblong of *shari*, another word for vinegar rice like *sushimeshi* or *sumeshi*. This form of sushi emerged during the latter years of the Edo Period (1716-1864), when it was a sort of accessible fast food that was eaten standing up at outside street stalls.

Nowadays, as we are more concerned about our health, sushi is becoming ever more popular, and it would be fair to say that it has won a place not only in Japanese but also in world cuisine.

[1] Please see page 84
[2] Please see page 94

目の前で職人が寿司を
握る姿が見られるのも
寿司屋での楽しみのひ
とつだ。流れるような
手さばきから作り出さ
れる寿司は、まるで芸
術品のように美しい。
One of the joys of
visiting a sushi res-
taurant is seeing the
chef preparing the
sushi right before
your eyes. The sushi
that the chefs seem
to conjure out of their
smoothly flowing
hands is as beautiful
as any work of art.

握り NIGIRI

　左手に用意した寿司ネタに山葵をつけ、右手に取ったシャリと一緒にふんわりと舟形に握ったひと口サイズの寿司。1貫（→P.154）、2貫と数え、1貫あたりの寿司飯の分量は10g前後。

　季節の旬のネタを中心に握っていく。ネタは生のまま握られるものもあるが、あらかじめ酢締め（→P.154）や昆布締め（→P.154）にしたり、ヅケ（→P.154）にしたり、表面を炙ったりするものもある。飾り包丁を入れたり、包丁の角で叩いたりするネタもある。

　さらに、できあがった握りにツメ（→P.154）を塗ったり塩を振ったりするほか、生姜、浅葱などの薬味を添えたりもする。

鮪 大トロ／Bluefin tuna *otoro*

The chef applies the wasabi to the fish in his left hand, then takes the rice with his right and creates a bite-sized piece of sushi in the shape of a little boat. The pieces are counted as "ik-kan[1]" (one piece) or "ni-kan" (two pieces) , one "kan" being composed of around 10 grams of *sushimeshi*.

The chef tends to mainly make sushi with seasonal ingredients. Although some of the ingredients are molded raw, others are marinated with vinegar (*sujime*),[2] packed between strips of kelp (*kobujime*),[3] marinated in soy sauce (*zuke*)[4] or lightly seared. Some of the ingredients are decoratively sliced or beaten with the side of a knife.

Some sushi is further dressed with a sauce, sprinkled with salt, or decorated with seasonings such as ginger or chives.

軍艦巻き GUNKAN-MAKI

　海胆やイクラのように形の崩れやすいネタを握るときの方法。通常の握りよりもやや小ぶりな箱形にシャリを握り、まな板に置いて山葵を乗せ、海苔でぐるりと巻く。シャリの上にネタを盛ったらできあがり。

This is a method for molding toppings that can easily collapse or topple over, such as sea urchin and salmon roe. The rice is molded into a box-shaped piece slightly smaller than usual, then placed on a chopping board, dabbed

海胆／Sea urchin

with wasabi and then wrapped with toasted seaweed (*nori*). Finally, the topping is nestled on top of the rice.

海苔巻き NORI-MAKI

　巻き簀の上に海苔を広げてシャリを敷き、芯となる具を乗せて巻いた、巻き寿司。太さの違いによって細巻き、中巻き、太巻きという。巻き簀を使わない場合は手巻きという。

Maki-zushi is made by spreading out nori on a bamboo mat called a *makisu*, on top of which rice and the topping is laid before being rolled up. It comes in different thicknesses: (thinnest first) *hoso-maki*, *chu-maki* and

カッパ巻き／Cucumber roll

futo-maki. *Maki-zushi* made without the use of a *makisu* is called *temaki*, which means "hand-rolled."

② 寿司の食べ方 How to eat sushi

　握り寿司は、手でつまむのが一般的とされている。しかし、屋台の立ち食いで手っ取り早いからという慣習に過ぎず、必ずという決まりもない。醤油をつけるのにシャリを浸してしまうようでなければ、もちろん箸を使ってもよい。

People usually eat *nigiri-zushi* with their hands. However, this is merely a custom that grew because it was a quick way of eating while standing at a street stall, and there is no hard and fast rule about using your hands. As long as you do not soak the rice with too much soy sauce, you can of course use chopsticks.

Lesson 1　箸の使い方 How to use chopsticks

　箸を正しく持つことは、和食の席での大事なマナーのひとつ。箸で寿司を突き刺したり、すくうような使い方をしないよう気をつけたい。

Using chopsticks correctly is an important part of the etiquette of eating Japanese food. Please ensure that you do not stab or scoop up the sushi with your chopsticks.

Step 1

固定するほうの箸を親指の根元に挟む。薬指と小指は軽く曲げ、薬指の第一関節の上に箸を置き、親指で支える。

Fit the chopstick that will remain still on the base of your thumb. Gently bend your third finger and little finger, placing the chopstick on the first joint of your third finger and supporting it with your thumb.

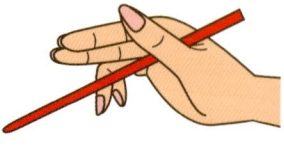

14

Step 2

もう一方の箸を親指の腹で挟み、中指の第一関節で支えるように持つ。人差し指は箸の上に軽く添える。

Fit the other chopstick in the bend of your thumb, and support it with the first joint of your middle finger. Gently place your index finger over the chopstick.

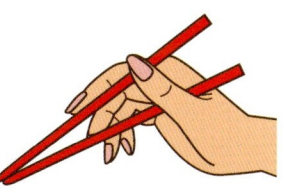

Step 3

人差し指と中指を動かして上の方の箸を上下に動かす。二本の箸を両方動かすのではなく、下の箸はしっかりと固定し、上の箸を上手に動かす。

Move your index finger and middle finger to make the upper chopstick go up and down. Try not to move both chopsticks, and neatly manipulate the upper chopstick while keeping the lower one still.

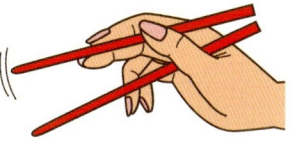

COLUMN

割り箸の割り方
How to use disposable chopsticks

左右に勢いよく割っている人をよく見かけるが、実はこの割り方はマナー違反。割り箸は右手で下側の箸をしっかり固定し、上側の箸を左手で持ち上げるように静かに割るのがよい。

You sometimes see people vigorously tearing apart the chopsticks from left to right, though this is in fact a rather bad mannered way of splitting them. The best way to separate the chopsticks is to firmly grasp the lower chopstick with the right hand and gently lift up the upper chopstick with your left hand.

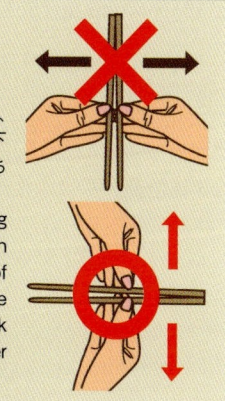

箸を使って寿司を食べる Eating sushi with chopsticks

　箸の使い方をマスターしたら、早速箸を使って寿司を食べてみよう。ネタとシャリが離れないようにしながら、全体をやさしく挟（はさ）めるかどうかがいちばんのポイントとなる。

Now you have mastered how to use chopsticks, let's try to eat some sushi with them. The most important point is whether or not you can gently grasp the whole piece of sushi while making sure the topping and the rice do not become separated.

Step 1　はねないようにゆっくりと醤油を醤油皿に注ぐ。

Slowly pour the soy sauce into the dish, making sure you do not spill it.

Step 2　箸の使い方（→P.14）で練習したように箸を持つ。

Hold the chopsticks as practiced in the "How to use chopsticks" section on page 14.

Step 3　寿司を軽く横に倒し、シャリと寿司ネタが離れないように寿司全体を挟むように持つとよい。

It is best if you can carefully tilt the sushi onto its side, and grip the whole piece without letting the rice and topping separate.

Step 4　寿司ネタの先に少量の醤油をつけ、そのまま口に運ぶ。シャリに醤油をつけると酢飯が崩れやすくなるので避ける。

Put a small amount of soy sauce on the sushi topping, and bring it up to your mouth. Try to avoid getting soy sauce on the rice, as this can make it crumble.

Lesson 3 　手を使って食べる Eating sushi with your hands

　手がベタベタするのが嫌という人は、箸を使ったほうがいい。しかし、江戸前の寿司はもともと手で食べられていたもので、マナーの面でも全く問題ない。カウンターに乗せられた寿司は、手でいただくほうがリズムもいいものだ。おしぼりとは別に、手ふき専用の布巾（ふきん）が出されるので心配ない。

People who don't like having sticky hands should probably use chopsticks. However, sushi was traditionally eaten by hand and doing so is not rude whatsoever. In fact, it builds up a good rhythm if you eat the sushi placed on the counter with your hands. There's no need to worry about your hands, as you will be given a hot towel and special hand wipes.

Step 1 寿司を少し傾け、人差し指と中指をシャリ側に添え、親指で寿司ネタ側を挟むように持つ。

Tilt the sushi slightly on its side, with your index finger and middle finger on the rice and your thumb on the sushi topping.

Step 2 寿司ネタ側に醤油を少量つけ、そのまま口に運ぶ。

Dip the sushi topping lightly in the soy sauce and bring it straight up to your mouth.

寿司は半分で切らずにひと口で食べよう
Try to eat the sushi in one mouthful rather than biting it in half

寿司屋で定番のテーブルセット
Common table setting at a sushi restaurant

　寿司屋でよく見かける食器や食材のなかには、寿司屋ならではの物がある。寿司を置く台は「付け台」と呼ばれ、一般的に漆などの塗り物が多い。

　刺身料理に用いられるツマの一種で、紫蘇や穂じそ、菊の花なども和食独特の食材だ。そのまま食べてもよいが、醤油に花弁を散らして彩りや香りを楽しむ食べ方などもある。

　There are a number of utensils and ingredients often seen in sushi restaurants that you won't find anywhere else. The wooden block upon which the sushi is placed is called a *zuke-*

お茶
Green tea

醤油
Soy Sauce

汁物
Soup

大根けん
Japanese Radish

紫蘇
Shiso

穂じそ
Flower of the Shiso

醤油皿
Sauce Dish

箸
Chopsticks

dai and is often lacquered. The garnishes frequently used in sashimi dishes, such as perilla, (known as shiso) and miniature chrysanthemums are all unique to Japanese cuisine. They can be eaten as they are, or you can sprinkle the petals on your soy sauce and enjoy the colors and fragrance.

汁物の飲み方 How to drink soups

寿司屋では食後に出ることが多い吸い物や味噌汁。お椀は左手で親指以外の4本の指をそろえて左手で持ち、親指は軽く椀の縁にかける。椀の縁に直接口をつけて、音を立てないように飲むのが正しい作法だ。

具材もスプーンなどは使わず、箸を使って食べる。箸を上手に使えなければ、スプーンを出してもらえるか聞いてみるのもいいが、和食の雰囲気を楽しむためにもぜひ箸を使って食べてみよう。

A sushi meal is often completed with clear soup or miso soup. Put all four fingers of your left hand under the bottom of the bowl and place your thumb, gently on the rim. Then hold the rim of the bowl right up to your mouth, and don't make any slurping noises.

Use chopsticks rather than a spoon to eat the pieces in the soup. If you cannot use chopsticks well it is worth asking for a spoon, but ideally do your best with chopsticks to preserve the atmosphere of Japanese cuisine.

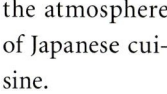

◈ 寿司の歴史

　紀元前300〜400年頃、中国の秦の時代、東洋最古の辞書の中に、魚を調理した食品「鮨」の文字が初めて登場する。

　日本の寿司の出発点と考えられているのが滋賀県近江の鮒寿司である。塩漬けにした魚を塩抜きし、ご飯に漬け込む熟れ寿司で、現在も各地で食べられている。やがて江戸中期になると箱寿司が登場し、稲荷寿司なども食べられるようになった。

◈ History of sushi

　The word "sushi" (鮨) to describe prepared fish first appeared in the oldest Oriental dictionary, compiled during the Qin Dynasty, around 300 to 400 BC.

　The first type of sushi in Japan is thought to be the *funazushi* (fermented sushi) of the Omi region, which is now Shiga Prefecture. This is a type of *narezushi* in which the preserved fish is desalinated and then packed in rice, and it is still eaten in various parts of Japan. *Hakozushi*[*1] (boxed sushi) emerged in the mid-Edo period when dishes such as *inarizushi*[*2] (stuffed sushi) also became widely eaten.

江戸時代のお月見を描いた浮世絵。「寿し」の屋台が出ていることが分かる
An ukiyoe woodblock print portraying a moon viewing party. You can see the sushi street stalls.

神奈川県立歴史博物館所蔵『東都名所高輪廿六夜待遊興之図』歌川広重(初代)

20　*1 Sushi in a wooden box, in which the sushi is made and pressed into.
　　*2 Sweet and spicy pouches of fried bean curd stuffed with sumeshi.

美味しい寿司を味わう

寿司の カテゴリー Types of sushi topping

◆ 赤身 *AKAMI* ·················· Red flesh fish

赤味を帯びた肉を持つ魚の
こと。おもに鮪や鰹など長距
離を回遊する魚で、寿司ネタ
の中でも特に人気が高い。

Fish with reddish flesh. This category main-ly includes fish that migrate long distances, such as tuna and bonito, and is a particu-larly popular part of the sushi repertoire.

◆ 白身 *SHIROMI* ·················· White fish

赤身と対照的に白身の肉を
持つ魚。鯛や平目など、短
距離を泳ぐため瞬発力に優
れ、身が引き締まっている。

This category includes varieties such as flounders and bream, which are muscular swimmers over short distances and have firm bodies.

◆ 光り物 *HIKARIMONO* ············ Silver-skinned fish

皮が青白く光る魚のことで、
寿司ネタとしては小鰭や鯖、
鯵などが代表的。塩と酢で
締めたものが多い。

These are fish that have a bluish-white glint, including shad, mackerel and horse mackerel. They are often marinated in salt and vinegar.

◆ イカ・タコ *IKA / TAKO* ··············· Squid / Octopus

イカやタコなどの軟体類。イ
カの王様といわれる障泥烏
賊などが人気の寿司ネタだ。

These include very popular ingredients like the bigfin reef squid, known as the "king of cuttlefish".

◆ エビ *EBI* ·················· Prawn

生きたまま殻を剥いて使う
「おどり」などが有名。エビ
本来の甘みを楽しめる。

Well-known methods of preparing prawns include the *odori* (dancing) technique, in which the shell is removed while the prawn is still alive, enabling diners to enjoy the inherent sweetness of the prawn.

◆ 貝 *KAI* ·················· Shell fish

鮑や赤貝など、寿司ネタとし
て古くから使われている。

These include abalone and ark shell, which have been used in sushi for many years.

◆ その他 ·················· Others

穴子やイクラ、数の子など煮
物や魚卵も人気がある。

Braised dishes such as sea eel, and fish roe are also popular.

赤身

AKAMI

Red flesh fish

鮪 大トロ

まぐろ おおとろ

MAGURO OTORO
Tuna, Bluefin tuna *otoro*

寿司ネタの王様といわれるホンマグロは、全長3m、体重400kgを超え、日本沿岸の鮪としては最大。とくに青森・大間の鮪は漁獲量も少なく、極上の一品とされる。なかでも大トロは「蛇腹」とも呼ばれ、なめらかでとろける舌触りが特徴だ。中トロとの間の「霜降り」は脂が全体に行きわたり、なめらかな口当たりだ。

江戸時代、鮪は下魚として敬遠され、特に脂身は江戸っ子の嗜好に合わなかったらしい。トロが珍重されるようになったのは、1960年以降のことである。

鮪はこのほか、濃厚な味のタイセイヨウマグロ、トロの多いインドマグロ、夏が旬のキハダマグロなどがある。

Bluefin tuna, regarded as the king of all sushi ingredients, grow to a length of over three meters and many weigh more than 400 kilograms. They are the largest tuna caught in the Japanese coastal area. The tuna caught in the seas off Ohma in Aomori Prefecture are scarce in number, and thought to be the ultimate in quality. *Otoro* is also sometimes referred to as *jabara* (which means folded up in a concertina), and it is usually extremely smooth, seemingly melting on your tongue. The part of the Bluefin tuna known as *shimofuri* (falling frost) is streaked with fat and has a silky taste.

In the Edo Period, tuna was avoided as it was regarded as *gezakana*.[1] Apparently the fatty meat in particular did not suit Edo residents' palates. It was not until after the 1960s that tuna started to become highly prized.

Other varieties of tuna include the densely flavored Atlantic bluefin tuna, the rich and fatty southern bluefin tuna, and the yellowfin tuna that is in season during the summer.

1月 JAN
3月 MAR
5月 MAY
7月 JUL
9月 SEP
11月 NOV

*1 Inferior, cheap fish.

FISH FACTS

- 学名／ Scientific name：
  Thunnus thynnus
- 主産地／ Most caught in：
  北海道・青森・長崎・島根・静岡／
  HOKKAIDO, AOMORI, NAGASAKI, SHIMANE, SHIZUOKA
- 地方名／ Local names：
  ホンマグロ、ホンマ、シビ／ HONMAGURO, HONMA, SHIBI
- 分布／ Distribution：
  日本近海、北太平洋の温帯地域など／
  Japanese coastal waters, warm areas of the North Pacific Ocean

鮪 中トロ
まぐろ ちゅうとろ
MAGURO CHUTORO
Tuna, Bluefin tuna *chutoro*

中トロはほどよい脂の乗りで味のバランスがよく、しっとりとした舌触りが抜群。

1年を通して寿司ネタ人気の上位を占めるほどで、鮪のなかでも特にファンが多いネタだ。

大正（1912〜26）初期頃まではトロという呼び方はなく、当時は寿司ネタとして人気があるわけではなかった。

「血合いぎしの中トロ」は脂が乗って、鮪特有のコクが味わえる。背ナカの中トロもうまい。

写真の鮪は青森・大間産。

Chutoro is moderately fatty, has a well-balanced flavor and gives a gentle sensation on the palate.

Used a lot throughout the year, it claims the most devotees of any sushi topping.

It was not called *toro* until the early years of the Taisho Period (1912 to 1926), and was not popular in sushi in those days.

Dark meat *toro* has plenty of fat on it, providing the unique rich taste of tuna. The toro from below the first dorsal fin is delicious.

The tuna in the photograph is from Ohma, in Aomori Prefecture.

鮪 赤身

まぐろ あかみ
MAGURO AKAMI
Tuna, Bluefin tuna *akami*

　赤身は鮪の背の部分に当たり、ホンマグロの真紅の赤身は、独特の香りと奥深いうまみが広がる。酸味と甘味、渋味のバランスを見極めるのが職人の技の見せどころだ。
　赤身を特製の煮切り（→P.154）に漬け込んだ「ヅケ」は人気の一品。天保（1830〜44）の末に、鮪の大漁があって江戸市中に出回った頃、日本橋・馬喰町で屋台を出していた「恵比須鮓」が鮪のヅケを最初に握ったとされており、その味が評判となって江戸の町に広まった。

Akami is found around the spine of the fish, and the deep crimson flesh of buefin tuna exudes a distinctive aroma and profound flavor. Ascertaining the balance of the fish's acidity, sweetness and astringency is the chance for a craftsman to show his skills.

Zuke, in which the red flesh is soaked in a specially prepared boiled down sake or mirin called *nikiri*,[1] is a popular ingredient. It is thought this method of preparation was initiated by Ebisuzushi, which had street stalls the Bakurocho in the Nihonbashi districts of Tokyo at the end of the Tenpo Era (1830 to 1844), when there were high catches of tuna and the fish could be found all over Edo. The flavor became popular and spread out across the whole of the city.

*1 Please see page 154

かつお

KATSUO
Bonito, Skipjack, Oceanic bonito

　春から初夏にかけて日本列島を北上する鰹(かつお)は、「上り
ガツオ」と呼ばれ、鉄をなめたかのような酸味と血の匂
いに、うっすらと脂(あぶら)が乗ったうまみは、強い生命力を感
じさせる。夏から秋に南下する「戻(もど)りガツオ」は、脂の
乗りもよく、また違った味わい深さをたたえている。
　一般的な寿司屋が鰹をネタに用いたのは、1960年代
中頃からのことである。江戸の寿司はヅケ（→P.154）
で完成されていたため、鰹のような鮮度が見た目に影響
する魚を無理に使う必要がなかったためらしい。
　薬味として、浅葱(あさつき)や生姜(しょうが)を乗せたりする。「戻りガツオ」
は炙(あぶ)りを強めにして供される。
　写真は宮城・気仙沼(けせんぬま)産。

The bonito that travels north towards Japan from spring to
early summer is called *noborigatsuo* (swimming north bonito),
and its rather metallic sourness, sanguine aroma and light coat-
ing of fat give one an impression of its enormous life force. The
bonito that head south in the autumn, known as *modorigatsuo*
(returning bonito) have plenty of fat on them, and have a rather
different taste.

Bonito started to come into general use in sushi restaurants
around 1960. As the sushi of the Edo Period was virtually all
zuke (and therefore already marinated in soy sauce) there was
probably no need to make any special effort to use a fish like
bonito, whose appearance is greatly affected by its freshness.

Chives and ginger are sometimes added as condiments to the
bonito. *Modorigatsuo* is served well-seared.

The fish in the photograph is from Kesennuma in Miyagi
Prefecture.

春〜秋
From spring
to fall

1月 JAN

3月 MAR

5月 MAY

7月 JUL

9月 SEP

11月 NOV

FISH FACT

- 🔴 学名／ Scientific name：

  Katsuwonus pelamis

- 🔴 主産地／ Most caught in：

  宮城・東京・静岡・三重・高知／

  MIYAGI, TOKYO, SHIZUOKA, MIE, KOCHI

- 🔴 地方名／ Local names：

  スジガツオ・ハタジ・マガツオなど／ SUJIGATSUO, HATAJI, MAGATSUO etc.

- 🔴 分布／ Distribution：

  日本近海、世界の熱帯・温帯地域／

  Japanese coastal waters, tropical and temperate regions of the world

◇ 鮪のいろは

鮪は今も昔も東京湾で獲れる魚ではもちろんないが、江戸時代末期に新ネタとして登場してから、江戸前寿司になくてはならないネタとして定着した。

江戸で知らない者はいないほどの人気店「與兵衛鮓」でも、鮪は当初は下魚と敬遠され、握られることはなかったという。

鮪を醤油につけたヅケを最初に握ったのは日本橋・馬喰町の「恵比須鮓」とされ、鮪は爆発的な人気商品となった。しかし、ここで使われたのは赤身だけで、脂の乗ったトロはまだ江戸っ子の舌には合わなかったのである。

現在、寿司ネタ人気の第1位に君臨している鮪だが、将来、この鮪人気が揺らぐことはあるのだろうか。

◇ ABCs of *maguro*

Tuna cannot now, and has never been, caught in Tokyo Bay, but the fish has become established as an irreplaceable part of the sushi repertoire since it first appeared as a new ingredient in the latter days of the Edo Period.

Even in the popular Yoheizushi restaurant, which everybody in Edo knew of, it appears that tuna was originally avoided as an inferior fish, and it was not used in sushi.

Apparently the first restaurant offering *zuke*, or tuna marinated in soy sauce, was Ebisuzushi, which was located in the Bakurocho in the Nihonbashi district of old Edo. Their tuna proved to explosively popular with the public, but in these days they were still using only red flesh as the fatty toro was not yet palatable to the people of Edo.

Nowadays tuna reigns supreme as the most popular sushi topping but will it continue to remain unchallenged in the future?

クロマグロ（ホンマグロ）
KUROMAGURO
Bluefin tuna

寿司ネタの王者。ホン
マグロともいう。北太平洋の
温帯地域に分布し、希少価値が高い。

The king of sushi ingredients. Also known as *honmaguro*. The fish lives in the warm areas of the North Pacific Ocean, and is expensive due to its scarcity.

メバチマグロ
MEBACHIMAGURO
Bigeye tuna

名前は大きな目に由来し、身体も太く
ずんぐりしている。日本における流通量は最多。

It takes its name from its large eyes, and its body is rotund and stocky. It is the most widely distributed tuna in Japan.

キハダマグロ
KIHADAMAGURO
Yellowfin tuna

漁獲量最多で缶詰の材料となるキハダ。

The catches of yellowfin tuna are the largest of any type of tuna, and it is used in tinned products.

ビンナガマグロ
BINNAGAMAGURO
Albacore

ビンナガは長い胸びれの小型種で身はピンク色。

Albacore tuna is a smaller variety of tuna with a long pectoral fin and pinkish flesh.

鮪の部位 The different parts of tuna

クロマグロであれば、全長3mを超える大きさのものも多い。当然、部位によって味や質が変わってくる。

頭側から尾の方向にかけて、上（カミ）、中（ナカ）、下（シモ）といい、腹と背でそれぞれ2丁の身が取れる。腹はカミに近いほど脂が強く、シモに近いほど脂が弱い。筋が強くなる大トロは腹カミ、中トロは腹ナカから腹シモに多く、背側は赤身が多い。値段に関しては、腹カミが最も高く、背シモが安くなる。頭はカマといって、DHAやEPAが豊富に含まれている。

Bluefin tuna can grow to over three meters in length. Naturally, the taste and textures varies from one part of the fish to another.

The fish can be divided into three parts from the head to tail – *kami* (upper), *naka* (middle) and *shimo* (lower). Two

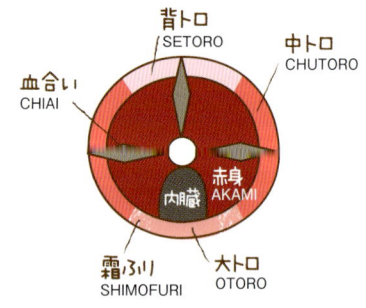

マグロの断面図
Cutaway of the tuna

背トロ
SETORO

中トロ
CHUTORO

血合い
CHIAI

赤身
AKAMI

内蔵

霜ふり
SHIMOFURI

大トロ
OTORO

blocks of flesh can be taken from both the belly and the topside. The flesh on the belly is progressively fatter towards the upper part, becoming less fatty toward the lower part. *Otoro*, the sinews of which are very strong, is mainly found in the upper section of the belly, chutoro is prevalent in the area from the middle to the lower part of the belly, while much of the red flesh is found on the spinal side. With regards to price, the upper part of the belly is the most expensive and the lower part of the spinal side the cheapest. The fish's head is called *kama*, and is rich in DHA and EPA.

鮪のブロックを切り分けていくことを柵取りという。板状の長方形の状態を、柵、あるいは短冊という。

生のクロマグロは、切った面が空気に触れるにつれて赤くなっていくが、冷凍物は逆に赤みが引いていく。

赤身とトロがある状態であれば、まずは赤身の部分を水平に切り取り、下部を座布団状態にする。それを垂直に切り出していく。血栓がある場合は、骨抜きなどで血管ごと取るときれいになる。柵取りしたものを切り分け、ネタとする。

Cutting the tuna into blocks is known as *sakudori*. The rectangular blocks are called *saku* or *tanzaku*.

The cut surface of raw bluefin tuna becomes redder the longer it is exposed to air, while on the other hand the redness lessens when it is frozen.

If a piece of the fish contains both red flesh and toro, first of all the red flesh is sliced off horizontally, then the remaining lower part is cut vertically into cushion-like slices. These are

then further sliced vertically. If there are any blood clots these can be cleared up by removing each blood vessel with tweezers. The strips of fish forming the *sakudori* are cut and used for sushi toppings.

クロマグロの主な産地 Where Pacific bluefin tuna are caught

　クロマグロは日本近海を回遊し、沖縄海域で太平洋側の黒潮ルートと日本海側の対馬ルートに分かれる。黒潮ルートでは3〜4月に高知沖、7月に三陸沖、9〜12月に津軽海峡へ。対馬ルートは3〜5月に壱岐、7〜12月に佐渡から津軽海峡を回遊する。9月からの本格シーズンには良質な鮪が揃いだし、多くは北海道や青森で水揚げされる。

親潮（千島海流）
リマン海流
対馬海流
黒潮（日本海流）

噴火湾　恵山
戸井
松前　苫小牧沖
龍飛崎　大間
泊沖
九六島
三陸沖
気仙沼　金華山沖
飛島
佐渡島　塩竈
境
銚子
銚子沖
対馬　萩
紀州勝浦
壱岐
土佐清水　黒潮沖
五島列島　日ノ御崎沖
油津　室戸沖
沖縄

Bluefin tuna migrate to the waters around Japan, and separate into two groups around the Okinawan waters– those that follow the Japan Current on the Pacific side, and those that follow the Tsushima route on the Sea of Japan side. Those following the Japan Current reach the shores of Kochi in March or April, Sanriku in July, and the Tsugaru Straits between September and December. The tuna following the Tsushima route arrive near the Iki Islands in March to May, and move to between Sado and the Tsugaru Straits between July and December. Good quality fish are ready when the fishing season starts in earnest in September, with the majority of the tuna landed in Hokkaido and Aomori Prefecture.

白身

SHIROMI

White fish

平目

ひらめ

HIRAME
Japanese flounder

　平目は千島列島から南シナ海まで広く分布し、旬は9月から翌年2月の産卵前。特に寒中の平目は「寒ビラメ」として、古くから賞賛されている。やや琥珀色に染まった透き通る白身は、脂が乗って身が締まり、くせがない。握りや刺身をはじめ、あらゆる料理に使われる。

　ひれの付け根にあるエンガワは、筋肉質な脂の甘味が口いっぱいに広がり、やはり寿司ネタとして人気が高い。

　鰈とよく似ているため、「左ヒラメに右カレイ」と言って判別されるが、これに当てはまらない種類もいる。

　写真は最も美味とされる青森・大間産。

Japanese flounders is widely distributed from the Kuril Islands to the South China Sea, and they are in season from September until they start to spawn in February. *Kanbirame*, the flounders caught in the depths of winter, when the seas are at their coldest, have long been sought after. The slightly transparent and amber-tinted white flesh is firm and fatty, but without any overpowering flavor. It is both served as sashimi and used in all sorts of dishes, including *nigirizushi*.

The sweet aroma of the muscular fat found in the thin muscle of the dorsal fin, known as engawa, spreads across the palate, and is very popular as a sushi ingredient.

Because flounder closely resemble halibut the two are identified by placing them on their bellies; the head of the flounder will be to the left and that of the halibut to the right.

However, there are varieties that do not fit into this test.

The photograph shows a lefteye flounder from Ohma in Aomori, thought to be the tastiest.

1月 JAN

3月 MAR

5月 MAY

7月 JUL

9月 SEP

11月 NOV

FISH FACT

● 学名／Scientific name：

Paralichthys olivaceus

● 主産地／Most caught in：

北海道、青森、秋田、山形、千葉、福井など／

HOKKAIDO, AOMORI, AKITA, YAMAGATA, CHIBA, FUKUI, etc.

● 地方名／Local names：

テックイ、アオッパ、オオクチカレイ、メビキなど／

TEKKUI, AOPPA, OOKUCHI-KAREI, MEBIKI, etc.

● 分布／Distribution：

千島列島〜南シナ海／Kuril Islands to the South China Sea

真鯛

まだい

MADAI
Red sea bream

鯛は、日本最古の歴史書『古事記』にも記述があるほど古くから食されてきた魚で、"魚"といえば鯛のことであった。日本で獲れる鯛は10数種類あるが、寿司ネタとして握られるのは真鯛である。

旬は冬場から4月頃までで、桜の時期の最盛期には「桜鯛」といって珍重されている。淡白でくせのない上品な白身は、しっかりと締まった身の充実感を確かめながら味わいたい。

握る際は、皮目に湯をかけて氷で締める皮霜造りにするか、皮目を炙ることが多い。皮下の脂がうまいのだ。写真の真鯛は愛媛・八幡浜産で、1.5kg〜2kgの天然物。

Red sea bream has been eaten in Japan since ancient days, as testified by its mention in Japan's oldest book, the Kojiki. There was a time when the word "fish" meant red sea bream. The sea bream caught in Japan consist of ten varieties but it is the red sea bream that is used in sushi.

The red sea bream season runs from winter to April, and that eaten at the peak of the cherry blossom season, knows as *sakuradai* is highly sought after.

The pallid, mildly flavored and elegant white flesh is firm and deserves to be enjoyed with a sense of fulfillment. When used in sushi the skin is generally given a splashing with hot water and then chilled on ice, a technique known as *kawashimozukuri* or else seared. The fatty flesh is delicious.

The photograph shows a specimen from Yawatahama in Ehime Prefecture, caught in the wild and weighing around 1.5 to 2 kilograms.

1月 JAN

3月 MAR

5月 MAY

7月 JUL

9月 SEP

11月 NOV

● 学名／Scientific name：*Pagrus major*

● 主産地／Most caught in：

愛媛、福岡、長崎、熊本、大分、山口、兵庫など／

EHIME, FUKUOKA, NAGASAKI, KUMAMOTO,

OITA, YAMAGUCHI, HYOGO, etc.

● 地方名／Local names：カスゴ、チャリコ、サクラダイ、ムギワラダイ、タイゴ等／

KASUGO, CHARIKO, SAKURADAI, MUGIWARADAI, TAIGO, etc.

● 分布／Distribution：

日本列島・朝鮮半島～南シナ海／

Japanese islands, the Korean Peninsula from the South China Sea

縞鰺 <ruby>縞鰺<rt>しまあじ</rt></ruby>

SHIMAAJI
Striped jack, white trevally

　日本の中部以南からインド洋まで分布。伊豆諸島の周辺で獲れることから島鰺、また若魚（<ruby>若魚<rt>わかぎょ</rt></ruby>）の体側中央に黄色い縦縞（<ruby>縦縞<rt>たてじま</rt></ruby>）があることから、縞鰺（<ruby>縞鰺<rt>しまあじ</rt></ruby>）の漢字も用いられる。

　特に夏の寿司ネタには欠かせない高級魚で、数あるアジ科のなかでは最も美味とされる。見た目は同じアジ科の真鰺と同様に青魚だが、鯛などの白身魚と中間的な味わいで人気が高い。

　銀色の皮目を残した乳白色（<ruby>乳白色<rt>にゅうはくしょく</rt></ruby>）の身を、さっぱりと生姜（<ruby>生姜<rt>しょうが</rt></ruby>）でいただくと、なめらかな舌触りのなかから、上品な甘みとともに鰺独特の青魚のうまみが広がってくる。

　写真の縞鰺は高知・宿毛（<ruby>宿毛<rt>すくも</rt></ruby>）産。

春〜秋
From spring
to fall

1月 JAN

3月 MAR

5月 MAY

7月 JUL

9月 SEP

11月 NOV

Striped jacks are found in the waters south of central Japan all the way down to the Indian Ocean. The word *shima* in Japanese can mean "island" or "stripe" depending upon which character is used, and their name is sometimes written as "島鰺" because they are caught around the Izu Islands, and sometimes as "縞鰺" because of the horizontal yellow stripe found on the younger fish.

This is the most delicious of the Carangidae family of luxury fish that forms an essential part of the sushi repertoire in summer. It is a blue-backed fish similar in appearance to the horse mackerel, but it is popular for its white flesh and taste which is in between seabream and horse mackerel.

The milky white flesh with its silvery skin provides a smooth sensation on the palate when eaten with ginger, and the elegant sweetness and the flavor unique to blue-backed fish spread out across your taste buds.

The photograph shows a striped jack from Sukumo in Kochi Prefecture.

FISH FACT

- 学名／ Scientific name：
  Pseudocaranx dentex
- 主産地／ Most caught in：
  九州、伊豆諸島、高知、千葉など
  KYUSHU, IZU ISLANDS, KOCHI, CHIBA, etc.
- 地方名／ Local names：
  オオカミ、コセ、コセアジ、カイワリ／
  OOKAMI, KOSE, KOSEAJI, KAIWARI, etc.
- 分布／ Distribution：
  日本列島中部以南〜インド洋／ Japanese Islands from the Indian Ocean

鰤
ぶり

BURI
Japanese amberjack

　鰤は成長に応じて呼び方が変わる「出世魚」。生後1年でワカシ、2年でイナダ、3年でワラサ、5年以上で60cm〜1mの鰤となる。春から初夏は日本列島沿いを北上し、秋から冬にかけて沖合を南下する回遊魚。

　11月終わり頃の北陸では、霰や霰とともに猛烈な風が吹き荒れ、雷が激しく鳴る日があり、これを「鰤起し」と呼んでいる。特に厳寒期の北陸で水揚げされたものは「寒ブリ」と冬を代表する魚として珍重されている。

　成長した鰤は脂の甘みに豊かな香りが加わって、うまさはこの上ない。写真は北海道・余市産。

The Japanese amberjacks are one of shusseuo (fish whose name changes according to their age). They are called *wakashi* until they are one year old, *inada* in their second year, *warasa* in their third, finally becoming *buri* when they have reached the age of five years and grown to a length of between 60 centimeters and one meter. They are a migratory species that move northwards through Japanese waters from spring to early summer, and return south from autumn to winter.

From around the end of November the Hokuriku region in the north of central Japan is battered by hails of all shapes and sizes and lashed by violent winds. Sometimes accompanied by roars of thunder, this time of the year is called *buriokoshi*, which literally means "waking up the amberjacks". The amberjacks caught during Hokuriku's cold snap are known as kan-buri"and are particularly prized as the fish that represents the Japanese winter.

Nothing is more delicious than a fully-grown amberjack, with the sweetness of its fat and its rich aroma. The photograph shows a Japanese amberjack from Yoichi in Hokkaido Prefecture.

秋〜冬
From fall
to winter

1月 JAN

3月 MAR

5月 MAY

7月 JUL

9月 SEP

11月 NOV

FISH FACT

- 🔴 学名／Scientific name：*Seriola quinqueradiata*
- 🔴 主産地／Most caught in：長崎、石川、島根、鳥取、千葉、北海道など／
  NAGASAKI, ISHIKAWA, SHIMANE, TOTTORI, CHIBA, HOKKAIDO, etc.
- 🔴 地方名／Local names：関東＝ワカシ→イナダ→ワラサ→ブリ　関西＝モジャコ→ワ
  カナ→ツバス→ハマチ→メジロ→ブリ：名前の変わる出世魚（→P.56）／KANTO RE-
  GION（EAST JAPAN）=WAKASHI→INADA→WARASA→BURI　KANSAI
  REGION（WEST JAPAN）=MOJAKO→WAKANA→TSUBASU→HAMACHI→
  MEJIRO→BURI：Fish whose names change as they grow（please see page 56）
- 🔴 分布／Distribution：北海道南部〜九州、東シナ海など／South HOKKAIDO
  from KYUSHU, East China Sea

勘八
かんぱち

KANPACHI
Great amberjack

　勘八の旬は初夏から夏頃。同じ仲間の鰤や平政と比較して高級魚とされている。東京では勘八が人気なのに対して、関西では平政が多く消費される。

　眼の上の黒い模様が上から見ると「八」の字に見えることから、間八、勘八の漢字が用いられる。

　寿司ネタには2.5kgほどのものがバランスがよいとされる。近ごろは九州や四国で養殖が盛んに行われている。写真は大分・佐賀関産。ほどよい脂が乗り、引き締まった身の淡いピンク色が美しい。

　品のよい甘みとしっかりした歯ごたえのある食感は、日本の夏の暑さを忘れさせてくれる味だ。

Early to mid-summer is the season for greater amberjack. The species is considered to be something of a luxury fish compared to the closely related Japanese amberjack and *hiramasa* (yellowtail amberjack). The greater amberjack is popular in Tokyo, while most of the yellowtail amberjacks are consumed in the western Kansai district.

In Japanese the fish's name is written both as "間八" and "勘八" due to the black pattern above its eye, which resembles the character "八", the number eight.

Fish weighing around 2.5 kilograms are thought to be of the right balance for use in sushi. In recent years there has been a surge in the farming of greater amberjacks in Kyushu and Shikoku. The photograph shows a specimen from Saganoseki in Oita Prefecture. It has just the right amount of fat, and the pale pink of the firm flesh is delicious.

The elegant sweetness and satisfying texture provide a taste that helps you forget the oppressive heat of the Japanese summer.

1月 JAN

3月 MAR

5月 MAY

7月 JUL

9月 SEP

11月 NOV

● 学名／Scientific name：*Seriola dumerili*

● 主産地／Most caught in：

九州、伊豆・小笠原諸島、高知、和歌山／

KYUSHU, IZU, OGASAWARA Islands, KOCHI, WAKAYAMA

● 地方名／Local names：

アカバナ、アカバネ、チギ、ハチマチ／

AKABANA, AKABANE, CHIGI, HACHIMAKI, etc.

● 分布／Distribution：

日本列島以南、全世界の温帯・熱帯海域／

South Japanese Islands, tropical and temperate zones of the world

甘鯛

あまだい

AMADAI

Tilefish

　京都や大阪では「ぐじ」とも称し、棒寿司にしたり、昆布締め（→P.154）、若狭焼き、蒸し物など、古くから高級魚として懐石料理などで扱われてきた。甘鯛といえばアカアマダイを指すが、「若狭ぐじ」が有名で、石川県以西の日本海側が代表的な産地として知られる。

　特に晩秋から春先の寒い時期に旬を迎えた甘鯛は、脂が乗って、文字通りほのかな甘みをたたえてうまい。

　昆布締めにする際は、魚の余計な水分を取るため、軽く塩を振ってしばらく置いてから昆布で挟み込む。これを切り分けて握っていく。

　最後に、細く切った昆布を巻いて供される。

Also known as *guji* in Kyoto and Osaka, tilefish has long been used as a luxury fish in traditional Japanese banquet cuisine, featuring in *bozushi* (rod-shaped pressed sushi), *kobujime*,[1] *wakasayaki*,[2] and in steamed dishes. *Amadai* usually refers to *akaamadai* (Japanese tilefish), with *wakasa guji* being famous and celebrated as one of the foremost fish of the Sea of Japan waters west of Ishikawa Prefecture.

The tilefish that reach their season during the cold months from late autumn to early spring are particularly rich in fat, and as their name suggests (amadai literally means "sweet bream") they are exude a delicious sweetness.

When used in *kobujime* they are lightly sprinkled with salt and left for a while in order to drain off excess water, then pressed between sheets of kelp. The fish is subsequently cut into pieces and used to top sushi. They are finally wrapped in finely cut kelp and served.

1月 JAN

3月 MAR

5月 MAY

7月 JUL

9月 SEP

11月 NOV

*1 Please see page 154

*2 A dish in which the fish is cooked without removing the scales, while it is brushed with a sake sauce.

FISH FACT

- 学名／Scientific name：
  Branchiostegus japonicus
- 主産地／Most caught in：
  長崎、島根、山口、福井、石川／
  NAGASAKI, SHIMANE, YAMAGUCHI, FUKUI, ISHIKAWA
- 地方名／Local names：
  グジ、オキツダイ等／GUJI, OKITSUDAI, etc.
- 分布／Distribution：
  本州中部以南／
  South of central Honshu

鱸

すずき

SUZUKI
Japanese sea bass

　鱸はセイゴ、フッコ、スズキと、成長につれて名前を変える出世魚。秋から冬にかけて産卵するため、旬は夏。北海道南部以南の日本各地に分布し、『古事記』や『出雲国風土記』にも登場するほど太古から知られている。

　寿司ネタとしては3kgほどの腹太のものが使われる。張りと弾力のある身はやわらかく、嚙むほどに甘みが広がってくる。わずかに皮目を残した握り姿が美しい。

　夏が旬の鱸に対して、冬から春先にかけては「平鱸」が出回る。見た目は鱸にそっくりだが、鱸より平べったい身体をした高級魚。身はしっかりとして歯ごたえがあり、うまみに満ちている。

Japanese sea bass is another *shusseuo*, or fish whose name changes as it grows: from *seigo* to *fukko* to *suzuki*. As the fish spawn from autumn to winter, they are best eaten in summer. The fish are distributed throughout Japanese waters south of Hokkaido, and have been known for so long that they are even mentioned in the Kojiki and Izumonokuni Fudoki, the oldest and third oldest known chronicles in Japan.

Stout specimens weighing around 3 kilograms are used for sushi. The firm and springy flesh is soft and tastes sweeter the more you chew it. It looks very attractive with just a mere hint of the skin left on.

In contrast to the Japanese sea bass, a summer fish, the *hira-suzuki* (blackfin sea bass) appears from winter to spring. While it looks almost exactly the same as the Japanese sea bass, it is a luxury fish with a flattish body. The firm flesh has a good texture and is full of flavor.

1月 JAN

3月 MAR

5月 MAY

7月 JUL

9月 SEP

11月 NOV

FISH FACT

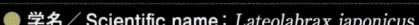

● 学名／Scientific name：*Lateolabrax japonicus*

● 産地／Most caught in：千葉、兵庫、神奈川、愛知、愛媛、福岡／

CHIBA, HYOGO, KANAGAWA, AICHI, EHIME, FUKUOKA

● 地方名／Local names： 関東＝コッパ→ハラク→セイゴ、デキ→フッコ、マダカ→

スズキ：名前の変わる出世魚（→ P.56）／

KOPPA → HARAKU → SEIGO, DEKI → FUKKO, MADAKA → SUZUKI：

Fish whose names change as they grow（please see page 56）

● 分布／Distribution：

北海道南部以南の日本各地沿岸、朝鮮半島南部／

Around Japan coast of South HOKKAIDO, South Korean peninsula

皮剥

かわはぎ

KAWAHAGI
Threadsail filefish

　代表的な磯の魚で、関西や四国ではハゲと呼ばれている。

　食べるときには頭のほうから皮を剥ぐため、「皮剥」の名がついたとされる。海釣りファンなら、たいていの人は釣ったことがあるおなじみの魚でもある。

　10月から11月ともなると、皮剥の肝はうまさを増してくる。透明感と張りのある身に、とろける肝と浅葱、紅葉おろしを乗せてポン酢をひと振り。

　適度な脂を含んだ身は、淡白ながらも奥深い甘みに満ちている。

　肝のあしらいはお好みに合わせ、写真のように乗せない場合もある。写真は神奈川・松輪の皮剥。

This typical inshore fish is called *hage* in the Kansai region and Shikoku.

The name *kawahagi* (skin-stripped) derives from the practice of removing the skin from the head downwards before eating. It is a familiar fish that most sea fishing fanatics have managed to catch at one time or another.

The liver of the fish becomes increasingly tasty during October and November. The firm, transparent flesh and melt-iin-your-mouth liver are garnished with chives and grated radish and red pepper, and sprinkled with ponzu, a citrusy soy sauce.

The flesh and its perfect balance of fat exude a subtle but profound sweetness.

It is sometimes served without seasonings, as in the photograph, which shows a thread-sail filefish from Matsuwa in Kanagawa Prefecture.

1月 JAN

3月 MAR

5月 MAY

7月 JUL

9月 SEP

11月 NOV

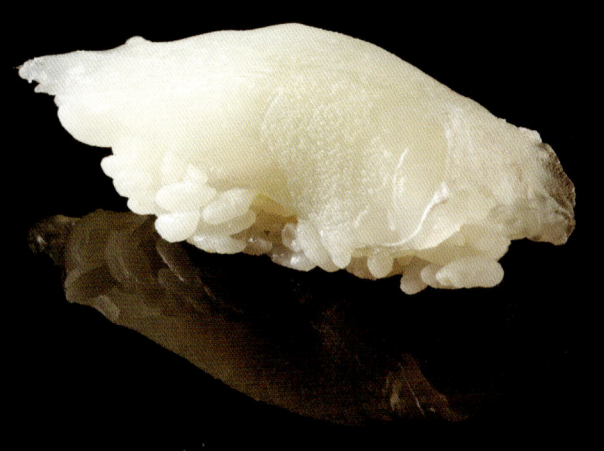

F I S H   F A C T

- 学名／ Scientific name：

  Stephanolepis cirrhifer

- 主産地／ Most caught in：

  九州、東京、神奈川、静岡／

  KYUSHU, TOKYO, KANAGAWA, SHIZUOKA

- 地方名／ Local names：

  ハゲ、カイ、カワムキなど／ HAGE, KAI, KAWAMUKI, etc.

- 分布／ Distribution：

  北海道以南、東シナ海／

  South of HOKKAIDO, East China Sea

鱚 きす

KISU
Sillago

　透明感のある飴色に輝くスマートな身体の鱚は、寿司ネタはもちろん、刺身や天ぷら、フライなどさまざまな方法で調理される。

　鱚といえば、一般的には白鱚を指す。脂肪分が非常に少なく、実に淡白。あっさりとした鱚のうまみをさらに引き出すため、握りでは昆布締めにすることが多い。

　昆布締めの方法は、軽く塩を振ってから洗い、水気を切ったら昆布で挟んでおく。皮はていねいに剥がし、最後に細く切った昆布を巻く。

　鱚の上品な味わいを引き締めるため、酢締め(→P.154)にする場合もある。

　写真の鱚は千葉・富津産。

春〜夏
From spring
to summer

1月 JAN

3月 MAR

5月 MAY

7月 JUL

9月 SEP

11月 NOV

The sillago is a trim little fish that has a transparent amber glow, and is popular not only in sushi but also fried, in tempura, and in many other dishes.

The term kisu generally refers to *shirogisu* (Japanese sillago). The fat content of the fish is extremely low, and it has a decidedly simple taste. In order to bring out the subtle flavor of the fish it is often served in the kobujime style at sushi restaurants.

The kobujime method consists of washing the fish after lightly sprinkling it with salt, and then sandwiching it between sheets of kelp when some of water has been drawn out. The skin is then carefully removed, and wrapped in fine strips of kelp.

At other times vinegar is added, which brings out the elegant taste of this fish.

The photograph shows a sillago from Futtsu in Chiba Prefecture.

FISH FACT

● 学名／Scientific name：*Sillago japonica*

● 主産地／Most caught in：

九州、神奈川、静岡、愛知など／

KYUSHU, KANAGAWA, SHIZUOKA, AICHI, etc.

● 地方名／Local names：

キスゴ、シロギス、マギス、ヒジタタキ等／

KISUGO, SHIROGISU, MAGISU, HIJITATAKI, etc.

● 分布／Distribution：

北海道南部から九州、朝鮮半島、フィリピン／

Sub-Hokkaido to KYUSHU, Korean Peninsula, Philippines

鯒 こち KOCHI
Flathead

　大きい頭に黄褐色の身体は、とても器量のいい魚とはいえない。しかし、ほとんど無色に透き通った身はしっかりと引き締まり、淡白なうまみを味わえる。

　旬は6月から8月で、特に初夏がいい。「夏の河豚」などと称されるだけあって、コリコリした歯ごたえとさっぱりした味わいが、涼感を呼ぶ。

　南日本の近海に多く、内湾や河口の砂泥地に生息している。写真の鯒は、神奈川・小柴産。

The flathead, with its big head and yellowish brown body, could hardly be described as a good-looking fish. However, its virtually colorless and transparent flesh is firm and has a light taste.

The fish is in season from June to August, and those caught in early summer are particularly good. Sometimes known as the summer blowfish, or the Japanese delicacy known as *fugu*, its chewy texture and clean taste deliver a cool sensation.

Many flatheads are found in the waters close to the southern coast of Japan, where they inhabit the shallow mudflats of bays and estuaries. The photograph is a flathead from Koshiba in Kanagawa Prefecture.

1月 JAN

3月 MAR

5月 MAY

7月 JUL

9月 SEP

11月 NOV

眞子鰈

まこがれい

MAKOGAREI

Marbled flounder

夏場の旬が多いとされる鰈だが、眞子鰈に限っては、冬場が旬となる。カレイ類は日本近海だけでも数十種類と多く、最も美味とされているのが眞子鰈である。

緻密な肉質は意外にもやわらかく、心地よい歯ごたえとともに豊かな甘みが広がってくる。

大分県日出町沿岸で獲れる「城下かれい」が有名で、高値で取引される。「銀座 久兵衛」では1.5kgほどのものを仕入れる。写真は千葉・竹岡産。

Flounder tend to be thought of as a summer fish, but the marbled flounder is also in season during the winter. Varieties of right eye flounders account for dozens of species found in the waters around Japan, and it is the marbled flounder that is regarded as the most delicious.

The quality of its closely packed flesh is in fact surprisingly soft, giving a pleasant texture and spreading out a harmonious sweetness across the palate.

The *shiroshita karei* caught on the coast off Oita Prefecture's Hijimachi is well-known and sells for high prices. The famous Ginza Kyubey restaurant uses fish that weigh 1.5 kilograms. The sole in the photograph is from Takeoka in Chiba Prefecture.

秋〜春
From fall to spring

1月 JAN

3月 MAR

5月 MAY

7月 JUL

9月 SEP

11月 NOV

◆ 出世魚って何？

　日本では江戸時代まで中国の風習を真似て、武士や学者は元服<ruby>元服<rt>げんぷく</rt></ruby>や出世に伴って新たな名を授かる習慣があった。これになぞらえ、稚魚から成魚までの成長に従って異なる名前で呼ばれる魚を「出世魚」という。縁起がよいとされ、祝いの席で使われる。寿司ネタでは<ruby>鰤<rt>ぶり</rt></ruby>や<ruby>鱸<rt>すずき</rt></ruby>が代表的。

　成魚以外の成長段階の名前は標準化が行われていないため、呼び方は地方によって実にまちまちである。

◆ What is *shusseuo*?

　Until the Edo Period Japan followed some Chinese customs, one of which was to give new names to warriors or scholars when they came of age or rose to prominence. In the same way, some fish, known as *shusseuo*, are given different names as they mature from young fish to adult fish. These fish are regarded as being lucky, and are often eaten on celebratory occasions. Examples of such fish used for sushi are the Japanese amberjack and Japanese sea bass.

　Since there has been no attempt to standardize the names for the various stages of maturity, they actually vary from one region to another.

◆出世魚ブリの呼び名の変化
Different names for amberjack through its life

10～20cm	20～30cm	40～60cm	70cm
ワカシ WAKASHI	イナダ INADA	ワラサ WARASA	ブリ BURI

関東地方での代表的な呼び名の一例
Examples of frequently used names in the Kanto region

光り物

HIKARIMONO

Silver - skinned fish

鯵 あじ

AJI
Horse mackerel

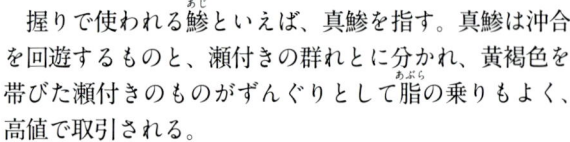

　握りで使われる鯵といえば、真鯵を指す。真鯵は沖合を回遊するものと、瀬付きの群れとに分かれ、黄褐色を帯びた瀬付きのものがずんぐりとして脂の乗りもよく、高値で取引される。

　寿司ネタ向きの小ぶりなものは、特に初夏がいい。

　昔は塩と酢で締め、皮付きのまま握るのが常道だったが、現在は皮を剥き、生のまま、鯵本来のうまみと食感を活かして握るのが一般的になっている。

　大分・佐賀関沖の「速吸の瀬戸」という海域で一本釣りされる真鯵は「関アジ」と呼ばれ、高級ブランドとして珍重される。写真は大阪・大阪湾産の鯵。

Maaji, is the most often used type of horse mackerel used in sushi. Japanese horse mackerel are divided into two groups – those that migrate around the offshore waters, and those that create schools in rapid current. Those in the latter group, with their yellowish-brown coloring, are stocky and packed with fat. They reach high prices at market.

The smaller horse mackerel that are suited to use in sushi areat their best in early summer.

In the old days the fish were usually salted and vinegared and used in sushi with their skins intact, but nowadays the skin is removed and the fish eaten without other flavourings in order to bring out their typical taste and texture.

The Japanese horse mackerel caught with the pole-and-line fishing technique in the waters known as *hayasui no seto* off the coast of Oita Prefecture's Saganoseki, is called *seki aji*, and is highly sought after as a luxury fish. The fish in the photograph is a horse mackerel from Osaka Bay in Osaka Prefecture.

FISH FACT

● 学名／Scientific name：*Trachurus japonicus*

● 主産地／Most caught in：

大分、長崎、島根、愛媛、福岡、山口、鹿児島など／

OITA, NAGASAKI, SHIMANE, EHIME, FUKUOKA,

YAMAGUCHI, KAGOSHIMA, etc.

● 地方名／Local names：

クロアジ、キアジ、ノドグロ／

KUROAJI, KIAJI, NODOGURO

● 分布／Distribution：

北海道南部から東シナ海／Sub-HOKKAIDO to East China Sea

鯖 _{さば}

SABA
Mackerel

鯖_{さば}は古来より日本人に馴染みの深い魚。脂肪分が多く鮮度落ちが早いため、握りの場合、塩と酢で締めて使われるのが一般的である。

写真の鯖は神奈川・松輪_{まつわ}産。「松輪サバ」は、大分・佐賀関産の「関サバ」と並び、高級鯖のブランド品として知られている。

やはり伝統的な一本釣り漁法で、極力人の手に触れないようにして運ばれ、生食にも耐えられるほどの鮮度管理がされている。

7月以降は脂_{あぶら}が乗って最高の時期とされるが、漁獲量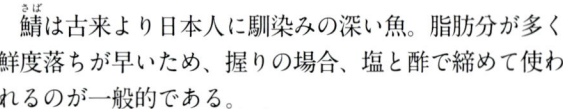が少ないだけに、別名「黄金_{しょうが}の鯖」と呼ばれる。

生姜かニンニクを添えて供されることが多い。

Japanese people have had a deep connection with the mackerel since ancient times. Because the fish are very fatty and tend to spoil quickly, they are generally salted and vinegared when used in sushi.

The photograph shows a mackerel from Matsuwa in Kanagawa Prefecture. *Matsuwa saba* is famed as a luxury fish that rivals the *seki saba* caught in Saganoseki, Oita Prefecture.

The fish is caught using the traditional pole-and-line technique. The fisherman are extremely careful not to touch the mackerel as this can cause it to spoil more quickly, and they handle the fish so as to assure the utmost freshness.

The fish are thought to be at their fattest and tastiest from July onwards, and the fish caught at this time of year when the catch is small are known as ougon saba, literally "golden mackerel".

The fish are often served garnished with ginger and garlic.

1月 JAN
3月 MAR
5月 MAY
7月 JUL
9月 SEP
11月 NOV

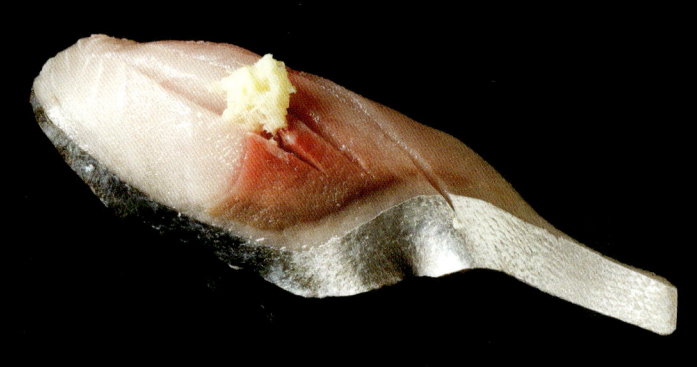

FISH FACT

● 学名／Scientific name：*Scomber japonicus*

● 主産地／Most caught in：

神奈川、長崎、茨城、静岡、三重／

KANAGAWA, NAGASAKI, IBARAKI, SHIZUOKA, MIE

● 地方名／Local names：

ホンサバ、ヒラサバ、ヒラス、タックリほか／

HONSABA, HIRASABA, HIRASU, TAKKURI, etc.

● 分布／Distribution：

日本近海、世界の亜熱帯・熱帯海域／

Japanese coastal waters, subtropical zone and tropical oceans in the world

小鰭
こはだ

KOHADA
Mid-sized konoshiro gizzard shad

　　光り物の寿司のなかでも筆頭に挙げられる小鰭。
　　美しい銀色の肌に脂を乗せて輝く小鰭は、塩と酢で締めることによって、寿司ネタとして新たな命を吹き込まれることになる。季節や大きさ、産地、脂の乗りなど、さまざまに変化する条件に合わせ、塩と酢の加減を見定めていくところに、職人技が発揮される。
　　初夏の走りに出回る小鰭の幼魚「新子」も人気の寿司ネタで、1貫に2匹づけで握られる。新子の初物ともなると、東京中の寿司屋が競って奪い合い、価格も高騰するが、それもまた、江戸前寿司の伝統的習わしというわけである。
　　写真は熊本・大草産の小鰭。

The gizzard shad is probably the prominent of the "silver-skinned" fish used in sushi. With its beautiful silvery skin and sparkling fat the gizzard shad gains a new life as a sushi topping once it has been salted and vinegared. The skills of the sushi chef are put to the test in adjusting the amount of salt and vinegar used, according to the season, size of the fish, where it was caught, how much fat is on it and other variable factors.

Shinko, a young gizzard shad that appears during the early summer run is also a popular sushi ingredient in which two of the little fish are placed on a single piece of sushi. When the first *shinko* start to arrive on the market, sushi restaurants across Tokyo compete fiercely to obtain the fish, making their price rocket, in another of *Edomae-zushi*'s long observed customs.

The fish in the photograph is a mid-sized gizzard shad from Amakusa in Kumamoto Prefecture.

1月 JAN

3月 MAR

5月 MAY

7月 JUL

9月 SEP

11月 NOV

FISH FACT

- 学名／Scientific name：*Konosirus punctatus*
- 主産地／Most caught in：
  神奈川、静岡、九州など／
  KANAGAWA, SHIZUOKA, KYUSHU, etc.
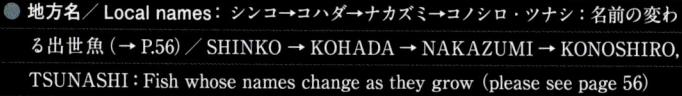
- 地方名／Local names：シンコ→コハダ→ナカズミ→コノシロ・ツナシ：名前の変わ
  る出世魚（→ P.56）／SHINKO → KOHADA → NAKAZUMI → KONOSHIRO,
  TSUNASHI：Fish whose names change as they grow（please see page 56）
- 分布／Distribution：
  東北以南の西太平洋、日本海南部、東シナ海、南シナ海など／Western Pacific
  below Tohoku, South Japan Sea, East China Sea, South China Sea

秋刀魚 さんま

SANMA
Pacific saury

　秋の訪れを告げる秋刀魚。背は青黒く、腹は銀色に輝き、柳葉の形で刀を連想させるところから、秋刀魚の字が当てられている。春から夏にオホーツク付近まで北上した秋刀魚は、秋になると三陸沖を南下する。

　落語の「目黒のさんま」でも知られるように、塩焼きは秋の日本の代表的な味覚。

　寿司ネタには、脂の乗りのよい秋刀魚を生のまま握るほか、塩と酢で締めたものも使われ、それぞれに違った味わいを楽しめる。

　ネタに飾り包丁を入れ、葱や生姜の薬味が添えられることが多い。写真は北海道・厚岸産の秋刀魚。

The Pacific saury is the fish that heralds autumn's arrival. Its spine glitters with a bluish-black and its belly with a silvery glint. The fish's willowy, sword-like shape is the reason behind the Japanese characters for its name, which literally mean "autumn sword fish". The Pacific saury, which heads north to the Sea of Okhotsk from spring to summer, turns south towards the Sanriku coast of northeastern Japan in autumn.

Pacific saury broiled with salt is a representative dish of the Japanese autumn, well known from the comic rakugo story of the *Meguro no Sanma* (*Meguro* Saury).

The fatty fish is used raw in sushi, but can also be salted and vinegared, and both provide different and enjoyable tastes.

Often the toppings are decoratively sliced, and garnished with chives and ginger. The fish in the photograph is a Pacific saury from Akkeshi in Hokkaido Prefecture.

1月 JAN

3月 MAR

5月 MAY

7月 JUL

9月 SEP

11月 NOV

● 学名／ Scientific name：

Cololabis saira

● 主産地／ Most caught in：

北海道、宮城、岩手、千葉、福島／

HOKKAIDO, MIYAGI, IWATE, CHIBA, FUKUSHIMA

● 地方名／ Local names：

バンジョウ、サイラ、サザ、サイリイ／ BANJO, SAIRA, SAZA, SAIRII

● 分布／ Distribution：

日本各地からアメリカ西岸にいたる北太平洋／

From around Japan to the North Pacific to the American west coast

針魚 さより

SAYORI
Japanese halfbeak

　春の訪れとともにうまさを増す針魚。細魚とも書き、ほっそりとした銀白色の身体に、長く突き出た下あごが特徴的な寿司ネタである。

　北海道から台湾の沿岸まで生息域は広く、南日本の内湾が主な漁場となっている。

　生臭みを消すため、かつては塩と酢で軽く締めて使われたものだが、近ごろは生で握るのが普通である。

　片身1本を輪づくりにして大胆に1貫に握り、生姜か山葵のどちらかお好みでいただく。歯切れのよい淡白な身は、爽やかで奥深いうまみに満ちている。

　写真の針魚は大阪・大阪湾産。

The Japanese halfbeak becomes tastier as spring approaches. A popular sushi ingredient, its name is written both as "針魚" (needle fish) and as "細魚" (slender fish) due to its slim, silvery body and its distinctively long, protruding lower jaw.

The halfbeak's habitat spans a wide area of waters from Hokkaido Prefecture to Taiwan, and is mainly caught in the inland bays of southern Japan.

In the past it was lightly salted and vinegared to hide its somewhat fishy aroma, but nowadays it is increasingly used raw and unseasoned in sushi.

The fish are cut horizontally, wound into bows that are dramatically presented on top of the sushi, and served with either ginger or wasabi according to taste. The great texture and pale flesh are packed with a refreshing and deep flavor.

The photograph shows a Japanese halfbeak from Osaka Bay in Osaka Prefecture.

1月 JAN

3月 MAR

5月 MAY

7月 JUL

9月 SEP

11月 NOV

FISH FACT

● 学名／Scientific name：*Hyporhamphus sajori*

● 主産地／Most caught in：

北海道から九州の沿岸／

Coast of the Hokkaido to Kyushu

● 地方名／Local names：

カンヌキ（大型）、スズウオ、ハリウオ、ヨドなど／

KANNUKI（KING SIZE）, SUZUUO, HARIUO, YODO, etc.

● 分布／Distribution：

北海道南部から朝鮮半島、黄海／

Southern HOKKAIDO to Korean Peninsula, Yellow Sea

春日子

かすご

KASUGO
Young sea bream

　春日子は関東の方言で、春に生まれた体長10cmほど
の小鯛。もとは血鯛の幼魚を指していたが、今では真鯛
や黄鯛の幼魚も春日子と呼ぶようになっている。朱色の
鮮やかな表皮がいかにも春らしい。

　春日子は鯛の幼魚だけに、生のままではうまみが足り
ず、寿司ネタに適さない。そこで三枚に下ろして塩と酢
で締めることによって、新たなうまみが湧き立ってくる。
歯ざわりのある皮がやわらかな身を引き立て、爽やかな
味わいを呼び起こす。

　なお、春日子は握りでは光り物に分類されている。
　写真の春日子は鹿児島、出水産。

　Kasugo is a word used to describe in the Kanto region, or
east Japan the 10-centimeter-long small bream born in spring.
The phrase originally indicated *chidai* (crimson sea bream) but
nowadays the young specimens of red sea bream and yellow sea
bream are referred to as *kasugo*. The fresh vermillion surface of
the young sea bream's skin is redolent of the Japanese spring.

　Being a young bream the fish lacks flavor in its raw state, and
is therefore not suited to sushi. By filleting the bream and then
seasoning it with salt and vinegar, however, the fish tastes completely different. The textured skin pulls together the soft flesh,
and creates a refreshing flavor.

　Young sea bream is classified as a silver-skin fish for sushi
purposes.

　The fish in the photograph is from Izumi in Kagoshima Prefecture.

1月 JAN

3月 MAR

5月 MAY

7月 JUL

9月 SEP

11月 NOV

FISH FACT

- 学名／Scientific name：*Pagrus major*
- 主産地／Most caught in：
  愛媛、福岡、長崎、熊本、大分、山口、兵庫など／
  EHIME, FUKUOKA, NAGASAKI,
  KUMAMOTO, OITA, YAMAGUCHI, HYOGO, etc.
- 地方名／Local names：
  カスゴ、チャリコ、コダイ／ KASUGO, CHARIKO, KODAI
- 分布／Distribution：
  日本列島、朝鮮半島〜南シナ海／
  Japanese islands, the Korean peninsula from the South China Sea

鰯
いわし

IWASHI
Sardine

鰯の種類は世界で300種類以上、日本近海だけでも20種類以上があり、真鰯と潤目鰯、片口鰯の3種が食卓でよく見かける種類。寿司ネタとしては真鰯が使用される。梅雨時の真鰯は良質な脂がたっぷり乗って、まさにとろけるような味わい。

足の速さはよく知られるところだが、流通での鮮度管理のおかげで、生でも握ることが可能となっている。ただ、小骨の多さは職人の腕が試されるところだ。

薬味として浅葱、生姜をあしらう。ネタに飾り包丁を入れるのは、シャリとの馴染みやすさと、食感を追求した結果である。写真は兵庫・淡路島産の鰯。

There are over 300 species of sardine around the world, more than 20 of which can be found in Japanese waters alone. The three varieties most often seen on Japanese dining tables are *maiwashi* (Japanese sardine), *urumeiwashi* (round herring) and *katakuchiiwashi* (Japanese anchovy). It is the Japanese sardine that is used in sushi. The Japanese sardine found during the early summer rainy season have high quality fat on them, and melt in your mouth.

Sardines are well known for spoiling very quickly, but thanks to careful management of their distribution route to keep them fresh we are now able to use them raw in sushi. However, the profusion of tiny bones in the fish provides a test of the sushi chef's skill.

The fish are garnished with chives and ginger, and then decoratively sliced is to improve both their adhesion with the rice and their texture on the palate. The photograph shows a Japanese sardine from Awajishima in Hyogo Prefecture.

1月 JAN

3月 MAR

5月 MAY

7月 JUL

9月 SEP

11月 NOV

● 学名／ Scientific name：

Sardinops melanostictus

● 主産地／ Most caught in：

茨城、千葉、静岡、青森、三重など／

IBARAKI, CHIBA, SHIZUOKA, AOMORI, MIE, etc.

● 地方名／ Local names：

イワシ、ナナツボシ、チュウバイワシ、オオバイワシなど／

IWASHI, NANATSUBOSHI, CHUBAIWASHI, OBAIWASHI, etc.

● 分布／ Distribution：

日本近海、北西太平洋／ Japanese waters, north west Pacific

白魚

しらうお

SHIRAUO
Japanese ice fish

歌舞伎の「三人吉三」で、女装の盗人お嬢吉三の有名な台詞に「月も朧に白魚の篝も霞む春の空」とあるように、白魚は春を代表する魚。隅田川の河口などで獲れる、江戸前ではごく当たり前の寿司ネタであった。

　特に2月から春にかけての白魚は子持ちで姿も大きく、最もよいとされる。こうしたいい時期のものは軽く湯通しして3〜4尾を1貫に握っていく。魚体が小さい時季には、生のままを軍艦に握る。かつては酢にくぐらせたり、蒸したりと、いろんな仕事が施された。

　頭部のかすかな苦みに続き、ほのかに潮の香を含んだ甘い身の味わいが広がる。

The Japanese ice fish is a typical springtime fish, as famously mentioned in the kabuki play "Sannin Kichisa", in which Kichisa, a robber disguised as a woman, says : "The spring sky with a dim mist over the moon and the icefish baskets." The fish are a firmly established part of the *Edomae-zushi* repertoire, and were caught in places such as the estuary of the Sumida River in Tokyo.

Full of eggs, the fish are at their largest from February to spring, and it is around this time that they are thought to be at their tastiest. The good fish caught at this time of the year are lightly blanched, and three or four are placed on top of each piece of sushi. When the fish are small they are served on top of pieces of rice wrapped with toasted seaweed, a shape known as a *gunkan*, or battleship. In the past they were dipped in vinegar, steamed and served in many different ways.

After the initial slight bitterness of the fish's head, a sweet flavor with a hint of the scent of the tide spreads through the mouth.

冬〜春
From winter
to spring

1月 JAN

3月 MAR

5月 MAY

7月 JUL

9月 SEP

11月 NOV

● 学名／ Scientific name：

Salangichthys microdon

● 主産地／ Most caught in：

福岡、青森、霞ヶ浦など／

FUKUOKA, AOMORI, KASUMIGAURA*¹

● 地方名／ Local names：

トノサマウオ、アマサギ、メソゴリ、シラユなど／

TONOSAMAUO, AMASAGI, MESOGORI, SHIRAYU, etc.

● 分布／ Distribution：

日本、サハリンから朝鮮半島／ Japan, Sakhalin to Korean Peninsula

*1 KASUMIGAURA is the lake between northeast Chiba from southeast Ibaraki

◈ 握り寿司の始まり

握り寿司の始まりには諸説あるが、江戸時代後期の文政（1818〜30）の頃、花屋與兵衛が握り寿司を考案した説がよく知られている。與兵衛は岡場所で夜明けまで寿司を売り歩き、儲けたお金で尾上町（両国回向院前）に小さな店を持ち「與兵衛鮓」の看板を掲げた。これが握り寿司の始まりといわれ、店は江戸中の評判となった。

與兵衛鮓の繁盛に影響され、江戸の寿司屋はすべて握り寿司に転向したとされる。江戸の風俗を伝える『守貞漫稿』には、握り寿司のネタとして、鶏卵焼、車海老、海老そぼろ、白魚、鮪、小鰭、穴子甘煮などを挙げている。

◈ The origins of *nigiri-zushi*

There are many stories regarding the origins of *nigiri-zushi*, but the most well-known is that Hanaya Yohei first offered it sometime during the Bunsei era (1818 to 1830) of the late Edo Period. He sold his wares in Oka Basho entertainment district of the city until late at night, and then used his earnings to set up a little shop in Onoecho (in front of the Ryogoku Ekoin Temple), called "Yohezushi." This shop became popular throughout Edo and is said to be the start of *nigiri-zushi*.

Influenced by the roaring success of Yoheizushi, all the sushi shops in Edo switched to the *nigiri-zushi* style. The Morisada Mankou, a record of the lifestyles in the Edo Period, mentions *nigiri-zushi* toppings including omelette, japanese tiger prawn, seasoned shrimp powder, japanese ice fish, tuna, Mid-sized konoshiro gizzard shad and sweet braised conger eel.

イカ・タコ

IKA / TAKO

Squid / Octopus

障泥烏賊

AORIIKA
Bigfin reef squid

　5月から7月頃までが旬となる障泥烏賊（あおりいか）は、漁獲量が少ないということもあって、数ある烏賊（いか）のなかでも最高級に位置づけられる。胴を覆う大きな円錐形（えんすいけい）のひれが、障泥（しょうでい）（馬の腹の両脇に下げる泥よけの馬具）に似ているところからこの名がついたとされる。ヒレを煽るように動かすことから煽烏賊（あおり）とも書く。

　純白で半透明の厚みのある身は、見た目と違って固いため、飾り包丁を入れて出される。それでも歯ごたえはもっちりとして、潮の香が訪れ、嚙みしめるごとに濃い甘みが追いかけてくる。まさに烏賊の王だ。

　塩し酢橘（すだち）て提供されることが多い。写真の障泥烏賊は三重・尾鷲産。

Bigfin reef squid is in season from May to July, and is the most exclusive of the many varieties of squid because of the small quantities caught. It is so called because the large conical fin that covers its trunk resembles an *aori*, a saddle flap that was placed over horses to act as a sort of mudguard. Because it often waves its fins like a fan, it sometimes written "煽烏賊" or "fin squid".

The flesh is pure white, translucent and thick, and is served decoratively sliced, as it is harder than it looks. Even so, it has a rewarding texture with a scent of the waves, and becomes slightly sweeter the more it is chewed. It is certainly the king of all squids.

It is often served with salt and a lime-like Japanese citrus fruit called *sudachi*. The bigfin reef squid in the photograph is from Owase in Mie Prefecture.

1月 JAN

3月 MAR

5月 MAY

7月 JUL

9月 SEP

11月 NOV

FISH FACT

● 学名／ Scientific name：

Sepioteuthis lessoniana

● 主産地／ Most caught in：

日本各地／ Around Japan

● 地方名／ Local names：

ミズイカ、バショウイカ、モイカなど／ MIZUIKA, BASHOUIKA, MOIKA etc.

● 分布／ Distribution：

北海道南部以南、インド・西太平洋の温帯・熱帯沿岸から近海域／

From south to southern HOKKAIDO, the tropical and temperate areas of the

Indian Ocean and the West Pacific

墨烏賊
すみいか

SUMIIKA
Japanese spineless cuttlefish

　名前の由来は墨の量が多いことから来ている。胴内に
甲羅状（こうらじょう）の骨があることから、関西など東京以外では甲烏（こうい）
賊（か）と呼ばれることが多い。身は厚く、ねっとりとして歯
切れよく、濃い甘みを持っている。
　夏から初秋にかけては、墨烏賊の子どもの「新烏賊（しんいか）」
が登場する。1貫に1杯〜2杯づけという愛らしい握り
との出会いは、初物好きならずともうれしいものである。
夏の爽やかな寿司ネタとして高値のつく人気の一品だ。
　墨烏賊はシャリとネタの間に海苔（のり）を挟んでいただくと、
また格別の味わいとなる。
　写真は鹿児島・出水産（いみず）の墨烏賊。

Literally "ink squid" in Japanese, its name derives from the
vast quantity of ink it contains. In the Kansai region and other
places outside of Tokyo it is also known as the *kouika* (shelled
squid) because of the shell-like bones along its trunk. The flesh
is thick, viscous but easy to chew, and has a dark sweetness.

Shin-ika (young ink squids) appears in the seas from summer to early autumn. It's not only people who enjoy the first
products of the season who will be delighted at the charming
sight of two of these little squids balanced on a single piece of
sushi. Used as a refreshing sushi topping in summer, this pricey
sushi topping is a firm favorite.

Eating the Japanese spineless cuttlefish sandwiched between
rice and toasted seaweed is another quite different culinary de-
light.

The photograph shows a squid from Izumi in Kagoshima
Prefecture.

1月 JAN

3月 MAR

5月 MAY

7月 JUL

9月 SEP

11月 NOV

F I S H   F A C T

- 学名／ Scientific name：
  Sepia esculenta
- 主産地／ Most caught in：
  愛媛、大分、山口、広島、福岡、長崎など／
  EHIME, OITA, YAMAGUCHI, HIROSHIMA, NAGASAKI, etc.
- 地方名／ Local names：
  ハリイカ、マイカなど／ HARIIKA, MAIKA, etc.
- 分布／ Distribution：
  関東以西、東・南シナ海／
  West of Kanto, The South and East China Sea

槍烏賊
やりいか

YARIIKA
Spear squid

冬〜春
From winter
to spring

1月 JAN

3月 MAR

5月 MAY

7月 JUL

9月 SEP

11月 NOV

　北海道から沖縄まで、全国の海域で揚がる槍烏賊。先は槍のようにとがり、胴は細長い紡錘形をしている。晩秋に出始めて、冬場に大きく成長し、甘みも強さを増してくる。産卵期が春のため、冬場が漁の最盛期となるが、沿岸に寄ってくる春を旬とする地域もある。

　やや薄手の身はやわらかで、くせのない上品な甘みをたたえている。うっすらと透き通る槍烏賊の握りは、実にすがすがしい美しさにあふれている。

　春先の子持ち槍烏賊は、雄よりひと回り小さく、胴の中に多くの卵を抱えていて煮付けにしてもうまい

　写真は千葉・勝山産の槍烏賊。

The spear squid is found in all Japanese waters, from Hokkaido down to Okinawa Prefecture. Its head is spear-like and its trunk is slender and spindle-shaped. The squid appear in the late autumn, and become increasingly sweet as they grow through winter. Since spear squids spawn in the spring the largest catches are in winter, but in some regions the spear squid season is during spring, when they swim closer to the shore.

The slightly thin flesh is soft and possesses a well-balanced and elegant sweetness. There is a crisp beauty to pieces of sushi topped with the faintly translucent spear squid.

The female spear squid containing eggs in the springtime are slightly smaller than the males, and is delicious served simmered with the eggs still inside.

The squid in the photograph is from Katsuyama in Chiba Prefecture.

FISH FACT

● 学名／ Scientific name：

Loligo bleekeri

● 主産地／ Most caught in：

五島列島、茨城、福島、青森、千葉、静岡など／

Goto Islands, IBARAKI, FUKUSHIMA, AOMORI, CHIBA, SHIZUOKA, etc.

● 地方名／ Local names：

サヤナガ、ササイカ、テッポウ、ゴウイカなど／

SAYANAGA, SASAIKA, TEPPOU, GOUIKA, etc.

● 分布／ Distribution：北海道以南～東シナ海・黄海／ From below HOKKAIDO

蛸 _{たこ}

TAKO
Octopus

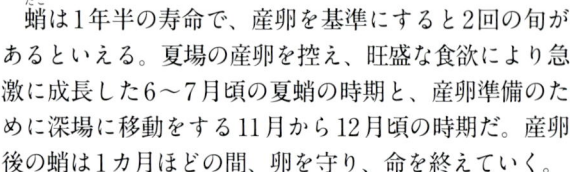

蛸は1年半の寿命で、産卵を基準にすると2回の旬があるといえる。夏場の産卵を控え、旺盛な食欲により急激に成長した6〜7月頃の夏蛸の時期と、産卵準備のために深場に移動をする11月から12月頃の時期だ。産卵後の蛸は1カ月ほどの間、卵を守り、命を終えていく。

蛸は表面がギザギザになるよう飾り切りが施され、包丁の角で叩かれて供される。それでも歯ごたえはしっかりとして、ほのかな甘みが湧き出してくる。

日本料理の世界では、やわらかく煮上げた蛸を桜煮といい、寿司屋でもつまみで出されたりする。

写真の蛸は神奈川・佐島産。

Octopuses live for just a year and a half, and are in season twice according to when they spawn. These seasons are in June to July before the spawning season in summer, when they have an enormous appetite and grow rapidly, and in November and December, when they move to deep waters to prepare to spawn again. The octopuses protect their eggs for around one month after spawning, and then die.

Octopuses are decoratively scored to make them look serrated, and are then beaten with the flat of the chef's knife before being served. They still retain their firm texture, and exude a faint sweetness.

Octopus legs gently simmered in soy sauce, mirin, sugar and other ingredients is called *sakura-ni* (cherry blossom simmered), and is often served as a side dish at sushi restaurants.

The octopus in the photograph is from Sajima in Kanagawa Prefecture.

冬〜春
From winter
to spring

1月 JAN

3月 MAR

5月 MAY

7月 JUL

9月 SEP

11月 NOV

FISH FACT

● 学名／ Scientific name：

Octopus vulgaris

● 主産地／ Most caught in：

瀬戸内海、九州、愛知、三重、神奈川など日本各地／

Seto Inland Sea, KYUSHU, AICHI, MIE, KANAGAWA and around Japan, etc.

● 地方名／ Local names：

イワダコ、イシダコ、イソダコ／

IWADAKO, ISHIDAKO, ISODAKO, etc.

● 分布／ Distribution：

世界の温暖海域／ Warmer parts of the world

◆ シャリ（酢飯）

　寿司の味を左右する米と酢。米はていねいに手早く洗い、ざるに上げて表面の水分を吸収させる。酢飯の米は粘りの強い新米よりも、水分量の少ない小粒の古米を使う。これを水を少なめにして固めに炊いておく。

　炊き上げた米に調味料を加えたものがシャリとなる。米酢に塩を入れ、酢の表面に泡が立つくらいに混ぜておく。飯が熱いうちにこの酢と塩を入れながらしゃもじで切るように手早く混ぜていく。できあがったときに人肌の温かさになっているのが理想的だ。砂糖を加える店もあるようだが、米と酢そのものの甘みを活かすため、砂糖を使わない店もある。

◆ *Shari (Sumeshi)*

The flavor of sumeshi or sushi rice is determined by the combination of rice and vinegar. *Sumeshi* is the combination of rice and vinegar that determines the flavor of sushi. The rice is rapidly but carefully washed, placed on a strainer, where it absorbs the water on the surface. Rather than glutinous fresh rice, *sumeshi* is made with older, smaller-grained rice and is cooked with less water than normal rice so it is firmer. Salt is whisked into the rice vinegar so that foam appears on the surface of the vinegar.

Salt is whisked into the rice vinegar so that foam appears on the surface of the vinegar. That is then mixed into the rice, using a flat rice scoop in a vigorous, cutting-like motion. The finished rice should ideally be at body temperature. Some restaurants add sugar, while others prefer not to, in order to maximize the inherent sweetness of the rice and vinegar.

エビ

E B I

Prawn

車海老

くるまえび

KURUMAEBI
Japanese tiger prawn, kuruma prawn

車海老は4月頃から10月頃まで、成長しながら名前を変えていく。大型のものを車海老、中型のものを巻海老、小型のものを鞘巻海老と称する。

旬は1年の中で初夏から夏の間の産卵前と冬場の2度とされる。

活きているままの車海老の頭をはずし、皮を剥いて握る。豊かに引き締まった最上の海老の身を生でいただく醍醐味は、他では代えられない味わいだ。

生をさっと茹でた車海老は色鮮やかに赤く染め上がる。芳醇な香りと甘み、身の締まりを確かめつつ食感のよさを味わうには、茹でたものもなかなかに捨てがたい。

写真の車海老は大分・姫島産の天然もの。

The Japanese tiger prawn's name changes as it grows from April to October. The large prawns are called *kurumaebi*, the intermediate specimens *makiebi*, and the small prawns *saya-makiebi*.

The prawns are in season twice a year, before the spawning period between early summer and summer, and in the winter.

When used in sushi the prawn's head is removed while still alive, and the skin removed. The exquisite flavor of the best prawns' firm body is quite unlike anything else. When rapidly boiled from raw the prawns take on a rosy hue.

This too is an irresistible way of eating the prawns, providing a mellow aroma and sweetness, and allowing the diner to experience the firm flesh and excellent texture.

The prawn in the photograph was caught in the wild in Himeshima, Oita Prefecture.

1月 JAN

3月 MAR

5月 MAY

7月 JUL

9月 SEP

11月 NOV

FISH FACT

● 学名／Scientific name：

Marsupenaeus japonicus

● 主産地／Most caught in：

愛知、熊本、福岡、大分、愛媛／

AICHI, KUMAMOTO, FUKUOKA, OITA, EHIME, etc.

● 地方名／Local names：

ホンエビ、マエビ、マダラエビなど／HONEBI, MAEBI, MADARAEBI, etc.

● 分布／Distribution：

北海道南部、オーストラリア北部、南アフリカ、インド太平洋沿岸／

South HOKKAIDO, Northern Australia, South Africa, The Indian Pacific coast

甘海老

あまえび

AMAEBI
Deep-water shrimp

　北国赤海老という和名の通り、全身が赤橙色をした甘海老。地域によって南蛮海老、赤海老など、いくつかの呼称がある。

　年間を通して水温の低い海域の150〜600m程の深海に生息。甘海老は不思議な生態を持ち、生まれて3年はオスもメスもなく、4〜5年目にオスとなり交尾して5〜6年目に雌に性転換する。この大きさで寿命は11年ほどとされ、産卵も3回以上行われる。

　小ぶりな甘海老の尾をはずして、2尾を1貫に握る。舌にやわらかい感触を残した後、豊かな甘みを残して溶けていく。子持ちであればそれもあしらっていただく。

　写真の甘海老は北海道・島牧産。

As its Japanese name, *hokkoku akaebi*, or "north country red shrimp", suggests, the deepwater shrimp is a reddish orange color. It is sometimes called, among other names, *nanbanebi* (western shrimp), or *akaebi* (red shrimp), depending upon where it is caught.

The shrimp lives in cold waters at a depth of between 150 and 600 meters. Mysteriously, it has no sex until the age of 3 or up. At around 4 or 5 it becomes a male. It is thought to live for eleven years at this size, spawning at least three times.

The tails of these little shrimps are removed, and two of them placed on each piece of sushi. After leaving an initially soft impression on the palate, the shrimp melt in the mouth with a residual sweetness, and should be relished if they still have their eggs.

The photograph shows a deep-water shrimp from Shima-maki in Hokkaido Prefecture.

1月 JAN

3月 MAR

5月 MAY

7月 JUL

9月 SEP

11月 NOV

88

FISH FACT

● 学名／Scientific name：

Pandalus eous

● 主産地／Most caught in：

北海道、秋田、山形、新潟、富山、石川など／

HOKKAIDO, AKITA, YAMAGATA, NIIGATA, TOYAMA, ISHIKAWA, etc.

● 地方名／Local names：

アカエビ、ナンバンエビ、コショウエビなど／

AKAEBI, NANBANEBI, KOSHOUEBI, etc.

● 分布／Distribution：日本海、オホーツク海からカナダ西岸／Japan Sea, from

Okhotsk Sea to Canadian west coast

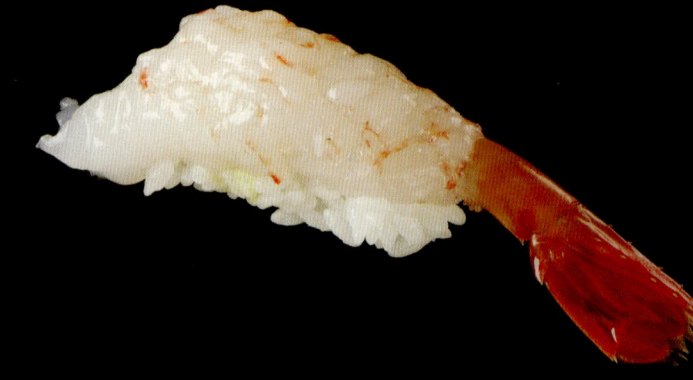

牡丹海老

BOTANEBI
Botan shrimp

春と秋
Spring and fall

1月 JAN

3月 MAR

5月 MAY

7月 JUL

9月 SEP

11月 NOV

富山湾で多く獲れるところから「富山蝦」の名もある。甘海老よりも浅い海域に生息し、北海道・内浦湾（噴火湾ともいわれる）では明治時代から漁獲されている。

甘海老と同様、タラバエビ科特有の性転換を行う。繁殖期にはまず雄として育ち、成長すると雌になる。

たっぷりと量感のある身は、食感を楽しめる上に、さらにねっとりとした甘みに驚かされる。写真の牡丹海老は北海道・噴火湾産。

The *botan* shrimp is also known as the *Toyama ebi* as so many of them are caught in Toyama Bay. Inhabiting shallower waters than the deep-water shrimp, they have been caught since the Meiji Period in Hokkaido's Uchiura Bay (sometimes known as "Volcano Bay").

The *botan* shrimp undergoes a sex transformation similar to the deep-water shrimp and other members of the caridean shrimp family. They start off as males during the breeding season, becoming females upon reaching maturity.

The plentiful flesh amazes not only with its texture but also with its dense sweetness. The *botan* shrimp in the photograph is from Uchiura Bay in Hokkaido Prefecture.

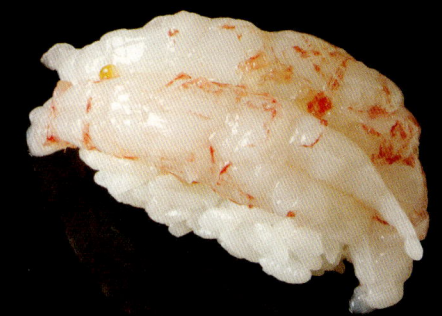

縞海老

しまえび
SHIMAEBI
Morotoge shrimp

　全身に紅白の縦縞が走る縞海老は、額角の棘があることから、正式名称を「両棘赤蝦」という。

　島根・隠岐から北海道沿岸の水深180〜500m程の海底に生息。同じ科に属する甘海老や牡丹海老と一緒に水揚げされるものの、量は獲れないため高価な海老だ。3歳から4歳にかけて、やはり雄から雌に性転換する。

　写真は北海道・増毛産の縞海老。甘海老と同じように握る。味も甘海老と牡丹海老の中間といった印象だ。

The shrimp's proper Japanese name, *morotoge*, refers to the red and white stripes covering its body and the spikes on its rostrum.

It inhabits the seabed at depths of between 180 and 500 meters, from the Oki Islands in Shimane Prefecture to the coast of Hokkaido. Although it is caught together with other members of its family, the deep-water and *botan* shrimp, the catch is small and the *morotoge* shrimp is therefore expensive. This shrimp also change from male to female between the age of three to four years.

The shrimp in the photograph is from Mashike in Hokkaido Prefecture. It is made into *nigiri-zushi* in the same manner as deepwater shrimp. The flavor is somewhere between that of deep-water shrimp and *botan* shrimp.

1月 JAN

3月 MAR

5月 MAY

7月 JUL

9月 SEP

11月 NOV

91

蝦蛄 _{しゃこ}

SHAKO
Squilla

　蝦蛄の旬は産卵期の春から初夏。雌は尾びれの内側に卵をいっぱいに抱いており、身の甘みはやや落ちるものの、卵の食感を楽しむという味わい方ができる。

　晩秋の脱皮の前ともなると、身がたっぷりと詰まった状態になる。殻のまま茹で上げて殻を剥いた身は、ふっくらとして、薄紫色に染まり、海老類とは異なる肉質で、香り高く食べごたえがある。

　カマキリの鎌のような捕脚の身肉を取り出した「蝦蛄爪」は甘みもひときわで、通好みのつまみとなる。

　海外産のものが増えたが、写真の蝦蛄は石川・七尾産。ツメ（→P.154）を塗るか、塩もしくは醤油など好みでいただく。

The squilla season is the spawning period from spring to early summer. The female's tail fin is packed with eggs, and while this to some extent reduces the sweetness of the squilla it allows diners to enjoy the texture of the eggs.

Before the squilla shed its skin in late autumn it becomes very fleshy. This flutty, lilac-tinged flesh is boiled in the shell that is later removed, and has a rewarding and aromatic flavor with a flesh quite unlike prawns.

Shakozume, literally "squilla claws", is a gourmet snack in which the raptorial limbs of the squilla – that resemble the scythe of a praying mantis – have been removed.

There is an increasing amount of squilla imported from overseas recently, but the specimen in the photograph is from Nanao in Ishikawa Prefecture. The squilla is eaten brushed with the *tsume*,[1] or else with salt or soy sauce.

1月 JAN

3月 MAR

5月 MAY

7月 JUL

9月 SEP

11月 NOV

92　　　*1 Please see page 154

FISH FACT

● 学名／ Scientific name：

Oratosquilla oratoria

● 主産地／ Most caught in：

北海道、愛知、岡山、熊本／

HOKKAIDO, AICHI, OKAYAMA, KUMAMOTO

● 地方名／ Local names：

シャコエビ、ガザエビ、シャエビ／

SHAKOEBI, GAZAEBI, SHAEBI

● 分布／ Distribution：

日本各地／Around Japan

◈ 山葵

　山葵はアブラナ科の多年生植物。「本山葵」と呼んで西洋山葵と区別する。主な産地は静岡・伊豆天城、長野・安曇野、東京・奥多摩など。寿司に使われるのは渓流や湧水で育てる「沢山葵」で、花の咲く３月より前の山葵がよい。寿司づくりに欠かせない最高の香辛料で、生の魚との相性が抜群によい。山葵を使うのは、寿司の味をより楽しめる上に、殺菌効果も期待できるという昔からの知恵でもある。

　山葵をおろすときは目の細かい鮫肌のおろし金を使い、茎の頭を垂直に立て、大きく楕円を描くようにすっていく。頭に近いほど辛みが強く、香りも豊かだ。

◈ Wasabi (Japanese horseradish)

Wasabi is a perennial plant belonging to the brassicaceae family. It is also called *honwasabi* to distinguish it from European horseradish. It is grown mainly in Shizuoka Prefecture's Izu-Amagi, Nagano Prefecture's Azumino and the Okutama district to the west of Tokyo. The wasabi used in sushi is the variety that is grown close to mountain streams and springs, and the plants are ideal three months before they flower. Wasabi is an essential part of sushi, the ultimate condiment and a perfect match for raw fish. In addition to enhancing the flavor of the sushi, it has long been known for its effective sterilizing capabilities.

Wasabi is grated using a very fine grater. The stalk is held at a perpendicular angle and grated in a large oval motion. This is because the wasabi becomes more pungent and aromatic closer to the head.

貝

K A I

Shell fish

鮑
あわび

AWABI
Abalone

　たいていの貝類が冬から春先に旬を迎えるなか、夏を代表する貝に黒鮑がある。昆布やアラメをたっぷり食べて、海の恵みをそのままに凝縮したような青黒い身の黒鮑。深い潮の香りを含んでこりっとした身は、清涼感を大事に生のままいただくのも格別だ。

　蒸し鮑の場合は、圧力鍋に酒と昆布だしを張り、約40分蒸し上げる。厚切りの身に飾り包丁を入れ、ツメ（→P.154）を塗るか塗らないかはお好みで。蒸した身はこの上なくうまみが増して、むっちりした歯ごたえもうれしい。

　写真は黒鮑で千葉・大原産。晩秋から春先まで北海道で揚がる蝦夷鮑も、磯の香りが鮮烈。

Though most shellfish are in season from winter to early spring, one typical summer shell is the *kuroawabi*, or black abalone. Gorging itself on various types of kelp, the bluish-black flesh of the black abalone seems to be a consolidation of all the bounty of the seas. The chewy flesh, which smells like sea, is fantastic eaten raw for its cooling sensation on the tongue.

The abalone can be steamed for around 40 minutes in a high pressure cooker with a broth of sake and kelp. Thick slice of flesh are decoratively sliced, and can be brushed with *tsume*[1], or not, according to taste. The steamed flesh achieves an unsurpassable deliciousness, and its dense texture is a further source of pleasure.

The abalone in the photograph is from Ohara in Chiba Prefecture. The *ezoawabi* variety of abalone found in Hokkaido Prefecture from late autumn to spring has a vivid scent of the seashore.

1月 JAN

3月 MAR

5月 MAY

7月 JUL

9月 SEP

11月 NOV

*1 Please see page 154

FISH FACT

● 学名／ Scientific name：

Haliotis discus discus

● 産地／ Most caught in：

岩手、宮城、千葉、山口、長崎／

IWATE, MIYAGI, CHIBA, YAMAGUCHI, NAGASAKI, etc.

● 地方名／ Local names：

オガイ、オンガイ、クロガイ／

OGAI, ONGAI, KUROGAI, etc.

● 分布／ Distribution：

日本海全域、茨城以南、九州／ Whole Sea of Japan, below IBARAKI, KYUSHU

蛤
はまぐり

HAMAGURI
Common orient clam

蛤の旬は春先から初夏。淡水と海水が混ざる河口付近から内湾に生息するものがよしとされる。

蛤は生では握らず、煮蛤とする。蛤を酒蒸しするか、さっと茹でてから、その茹で汁に醤油と酒、砂糖を合わせて漬け込むという仕込み手法を取る。

煮蛤は2つに開いて握る。ツメ（→P.154）を塗る、塗らないはお好み次第。醤油や塩でいただくのもよい。ほおばれば、心地よい歯ごたえに、豊かなうまみがほとばしる。写真の蛤は三重・桑名産。木曽三川河口域で漁獲される「桑名の蛤」は、江戸時代、徳川家康をはじめ当代の将軍に献上するのが慣例となっていた。

The common orient clan is in season from early spring to early summer. Those inhabiting the inland bays around river estuaries, where seawater and freshwater mixes, are thought to be particularly good.

The common oriental clam is not served raw in sushi, but is served simmered which is called *nihamaguri*. The clams are either steamed in sake or quickly boiled, and then soaked in resulting broth, along with soy sauce, sake and sugar.

The cooked clams are butterfiled and served on sushi. They may be brushed with *tsume*[1] according to taste. They are also good eaten with soy sauce or salt. Munching on a mouthful of these clams provides a pleasant texture and unleashes a flood of harmonious taste. The common oriental clam in the photograph is from Kuwana in Mie Prefecture. During the Edo Period it was customary for the "Kuwana hamaguri" caught on the estuary of the Kiso Sansen to be presented to Shogun Tokugawa Ieyasu and the other prominent shoguns of the era.

1月 JAN

3月 MAR

5月 MAY

7月 JUL

9月 SEP

11月 NOV

*1 Please see page 154

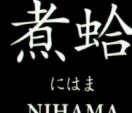

煮蛤
にはま
NIHAMA

FISH FACT

● 学名／ Scientific name：

Meretrix lusoria

● 主産地／ Most caught in：

愛知、三重、大分、熊本／

AICHI, MIE, OITA, KUMAMOTO, etc.

● 地方名／ Local names：

ホンハマ／ HONHAMA

● 分布／ Distribution：

北海道南部から九州／

From south HOKKAIDO to KYUSHU

平貝
たいらがい

TAIRAGAI
Razor clam

　平貝は、薄い青緑色をした殻の大きさが30cm以上にもなる三角形の二枚貝。内湾の砂泥で、尖ったほうを下にして海底に刺さるような姿で生息する。

　かなり大きな貝のため、寿司屋や高級レストランなどでしかなかなかお目にかかれない。

　旬は晩秋から初春の頃で、一般的にはタイラギという。帆立と同様に、食用とされるのは中心にある大きな貝柱のみとなる。

　乳白色に透けた身はみずみずしく真珠のような輝きを見せ、寿司ネタの貝としては、くせのない淡白なうまみか特徴。歯切れのよさでは帆立貝にも勝る。

　写真の平貝は愛知・伊良湖産。

The razor clam is a triangular bivalve with a pale greeny-blue shell that can reach over 30 centimeters in size. It inhabits the mudflats of inland bays, where it sticks its pointed end into the seabed.

As it is quite a large shell, you cannot usually find it outside sushi restaurants or high-end establishments.

It is in season from late autumn to early spring, and is generally called *tairagi*. As with scallops, it is only the adductor muscle at the center of the shell that is eaten.

The milky-white and transparent flesh has a pearly glow, and its even taste distinguishes it out as a sushi topping. In terms of the excellence of its texture the razor clam is superior even to the scallop.

The clam in the photograph is from Irago in Aichi Prefecture.

1月 JAN
3月 MAR
5月 MAY
7月 JUL
9月 SEP
11月 NOV

FISH FACT

- 学名／ Scientific name：
  Atrina pectinata
- 主産地／ Most caught in：
  日本各地／ Around Japan
- 地方名／ Local names：
  エボウシガイ、タイラギ、タチガイなど／
  EBOUSHIGAI, TAIRAGI, TACHIGAI, etc.
- 分布／ Distribution：
  北海道南部以南、インド洋、西太平洋／
  South sub-HOKKAIDO, the India Ocean, the Western Pacific

赤貝
あかがい

AKAGAI
Ark shell

　色鮮やかな赤貝は、寿司ネタの貝のなかでも最高峰に挙げられる高級ネタのひとつ。冬から春先の産卵前の2月から3月が旬であり、うまさの最盛期である。

　生息域は宮城・閖上が有名だ。

　注文すると、取り出した黒っぽい貝をガリガリと音を立てて殻を剥き、きれいにして飾り包丁を入れた身を、まな板に強く叩きつける。叩くことで身がきゅっと締まり、歯ごたえのよさが際立ってくる。職人の気っ風を感じる瞬間だ。

　写真の赤貝は大分・中津産。近年は各地で漁獲量が激減し、希少なネタとなりつつある。

Among the more luxurious sushi ingredients, the vividly colored ark shell is ranked at the very top of all the clams. The season for ark shells is February and March, just before spawning in the late winter and early spring, when their taste is at it best.

Yuriage in Miyagi Prefecture is one place famed for its ark shells.

If you ask for an ark shell in a sushi restaurant, the chef will take one of the blackish shells and tear off the shell with an audible ripping sound, clean and decoratively cut the flesh and then strongly beat it on his chopping board. Beating the flesh like this makes it firm and brings out the remarkable texture. It's a moment that reveals true craftsmanship.

The ark shell in the photograph is from Nakatsu in Oita Prefecture. The catch has plummeted in recent years, making it a rare sushi ingredient.

1月 JAN

3月 MAR

5月 MAY

7月 JUL

9月 SEP

11月 NOV

FISH FACT

- 学名／Scientific name：
  Scapharca broughtonii
- 主産地／Most caught in：
  岩手、東京、三重、大分／
  IWATE, TOKYO, MIE, OITA, etc.
- 地方名／Local names：
  タマ、ホンダマ、ホンアカ／TAMA, HONDAMA, HONAKA, etc.
- 分布／Distribution：
  本州中部以南から東シナ海、フィリピン／
  From south central Honshu to East China Sea, Philippines

海松貝
<ruby>海松貝<rt>みるがい</rt></ruby>

MIRUGAI
Pacific gaper, Geoduck clam

海松貝は、殻に収まらない水管の部分だけを開いて食べる。北海道から九州にかけての内湾に生息している二枚貝だが、水揚げ高は激減している。標準和名はミルクイといい、「本ミル」といわれるのはこの種である。

切り離した水管は湯通しし、水にさらしてから薄皮を剥く。コリコリとしっかりした歯ごたえに、強い磯の香りがあふれてくる。海松貝は鮮度こそが命だ。

本ミルの代用品として出回った白ミル（ナミガイ）も長く伸びる水管を食べる。今では圧倒的に多く流通しているが、こちらも高価になりつつある。

写真は愛知・三河湾産の本海松貝。

Only the siphon of the clam, which is very long and cannot be contained within the shell, is eaten. It is a bivalve that inhabits the inland bays from Hokkaido Prefecture down to Kyushu, the southernmost of Japan's for main island, and catches are rapidly decreasing. Its standard Japanese name is *mirukui* and the species is called *honmiru*.

The dissected siphon is boiled, and then the thin skin is removed after it has been in the water for a while. The flesh is very chewy and has a powerful aroma of the sea. Its freshness is paramount.

The extended siphon of the *shiromiru* (Japanese geoduck), another similar species often used as a substitute, is also eaten. Many of these are now in circulation but they too are becoming expensive.

The photograph shows a geoduck clam from Mikawa Bay in Aichi Prefecture.

1月 JAN

3月 MAR

5月 MAY

7月 JUL

9月 SEP

11月 NOV

FISH FACT

● 学名／ Scientific name： *Tresus keenae*

● 産地／ Most caught in：

愛知、東京、瀬戸内海／

AICHI, TOKYO, Seto Inland Sea

● 地方名／ Local names：

ホンミル、オオガイ、ミル、カラスガイなど／

HONMIRU, OOGAI, MIRU, KARASUGAI, etc.

● 分布／ Distribution：

北海道〜九州、朝鮮半島／

From HOKKAIDO to KYUSHU, the Korean Peninsula

北寄貝

ほっきがい

HOKKIGAI
Sakhalin surf clam

北寄貝は姥貝が正式名称。褐色の殻皮に覆われて全体的に黒ずんで見える。鹿島灘以北の太平洋、日本海北部から沿海州、シベリア沿岸まで分布し、浅い砂地に生息している。寿命は長く、30年以上。水揚げ高が日本一ということから、北海道苫小牧市の貝に指定されている。

北寄貝には、黒北寄貝と比較的安価な茶北寄貝があるが、寿司屋で使われるのは極上の黒北寄貝である。

身の舌触りはなめらかで、歯切れもよく、みずみずしい甘みが口中を満たしてくれる。軽く湯通しすると身が淡い赤紫に染まり、甘みが増してくる。

写真の北寄貝は北海道・長万部産。

Ubagai, which literally means a "granny clam" is this shellfish's correct name. This clam has a dark brown shell epidermis with an overall blackish appearance. It is distributed north of the Pacific coast of Kashimanada in Ibaraki Prefecture, and the northern coasts of the Sea of Japan, as far as the Siberian coast. It inhabits shallow mudflats, where it lives for around 30 years or more. It is designated as the clam of Tomakomai in Hokkaido Prefecture as it is thought that the largest catch of this variety is there.

There is a black variety and a comparatively cheaper brown variety of the Sakhalin surf clam, but it is the best black clams that are used in sushi restaurants. The clam has a smooth sensation on the tongue, a crisp texture, and fills the mouth with a fresh and juicy taste. Lightly boiled, the clams take on a pale magenta hue, and become even tastier.

The clam in the photograph is from Oshamambe in Hokkaido Prefecture.

1月 JAN

3月 MAR

5月 MAY

7月 JUL

9月 SEP

11月 NOV

FISH FACT

● 学名／ Scientific name： *Pseudocardium sachalinensis*

● 主産地／ Most caught in：

　北海道、福島、青森など／

　HOKKAIDO, FUKUSHIMA, AOMORI, etc.

● 地方名／ Local names：

　ホッキ、ウバガイ／ HOKKI, UBAGAI

● 分布／ Distribution：

　鹿島灘以北〜太平洋、日本海北部〜シベリア沿海州／

　From north of KASHIMANADA to the Pacific Ocean, from the northern part

　of Sea of Japan to the Maritime Province of Siberia

青柳
_{あおやぎ}
AOYAGI
Surf clam

冬〜春
From winter
to spring

1月 JAN

3月 MAR

5月 MAY

7月 JUL

9月 SEP

11月 NOV

　寿司ネタとしての「青柳」は貝殻を取り除いた部位を指し、貝としてはバカガイという。

　バカガイの名の由来には諸説あり、水揚げしておくと殻を開け、斧足（筋肉による足）を伸ばしている様子が口を開けて舌を出しているように見えるところからついたという説、「バカに多く獲れる貝」からついた説などがある。

　身はさくさくと歯切れよく、爽やかな甘さが広がる。写真は北海道・根室産の青柳。

　The *aoyagi* used in sushi refers to the part left after its shell is removed, while the clam itself is known as a *bakagai* (idiot clam).

　There are various explanations for the derivation of this unusual name. One is that it comes from the way that the appearance of the clam's stretched muscle hanging out when the shell is opened look like a mouth with its tongue sticking out, and another is that it is because they can be caught in idiotically large quantities.

　The flesh is crunchy and provides a refreshing sweetness. The specimen in the photograph is from Nemuro in Hokkaido Prefecture.

小柱

こばしら

KOBASHIRA

KOBASHIRA of surf clam

小柱は青柳（バカガイ）についている大小2個の貝柱のことをいう。大きいほうを大星、小さいほうを小星と呼ぶ。

むっちりとして弾むような身は青柳に負けず劣らず、さっくりと歯切れよく、甘みも強い。

小柱は江戸前寿司では生のまま、軍艦に握る。

小柱といいながら、写真のように美しく色鮮やかで、かなり大きな貝柱が握られることもある。

写真は北海道・根室産の小柱。

Kobashira are the two shell ligaments attached to the *aoyagi* (surf clam). The larger one is called the *ohboshi* and the smaller one the *koboshi*.

The dense and springy flesh is just as good as that of the surf clam, with its crunchy texture and pronounced sweetness.

In *Edomae-zushi* the surf clam ligaments are served raw atop rice wrapped in toasted seaweed.

As can be seen in the photograph, which show some from Nemuro in Hokkaido Prefecture, some beautiful and colorful ligaments are quite large.

冬〜春
From winter
to spring

1月 JAN
3月 MAR
5月 MAY
7月 JUL
9月 SEP
11月 NOV

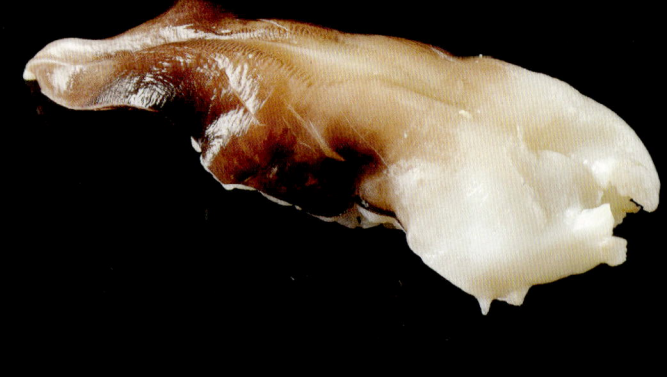

鳥貝

とりがい

TORIGAI

Cockle

鳥貝は、陸奥湾から九州の沿岸まで生息し、食用とする足の部分が鳥のくちばしのように見えることから、この名がついた。殻が極めてもろく、たいていは産地で剥き身にされ、ボイルしてから出荷される。

ふんわりとしてやわらかく、歯ごたえのよさを誇る鳥貝は、特に4月から5月にかけて獲れるものが身が大きくて厚く、甘みも強い。

墨色がきれいなものほど鮮度もいい。写真は愛知・三河湾産の鳥貝。

Cockles inhabit the coastal waters from Mutsu Bay in Aomori Prefecture down to Kyushu. The Japanese name for the cockle, *torigai*, literally means "bird shell," a name deriving from the bird-like appearance of their leg, which is the edible part. Their shells are extremely brittle, and are usually stripped and boiled where they are caught, before being sent to market.

The flesh is soft but has a good texture, and those caught from April to May are particularly large, thick and sweet.

The blacker the shells, the fresher they are. The cockle in the photograph is from Mikawa Bay in Aichi Prefecture.

春

Spring

1月 JAN

3月 MAR

5月 MAY

7月 JUL

9月 SEP

11月 NOV

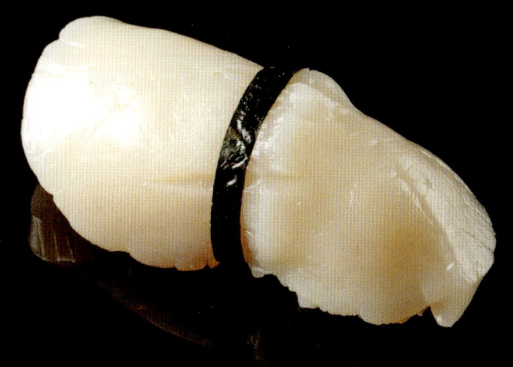

帆立
<ruby>ほたて</ruby>
HOTATE
Scallop

　寒冷な北の海で鍛えられた大きな天然の帆立は、養殖ものとは比較できないような強烈な甘みと、心地よくやわらかな食感を持っている。

　殻長12cmほどに成長した4年物の帆立は格別な味わいだ。太く大きい貝柱の部分が厚く切られて、ふたつに開かれた状態で寿司ネタとなる。

　ヒモと呼ばれる外套膜の部分は、巻物に使われたりもする。写真は北海道・野付産の帆立。

Tempered in the cold seas of the north, large wild scallops have a strong sweetness and pleasant eating texture that farmed scallops cannot compete with.

The taste of the 12 centimeter wide 4-year-old scallop is quite exceptional. Their thick and sizeable ligaments are cut into cut into thick strips and butterflied when they are used as a as sushi topping.

The mantle of the scallop, called a *himo* or "string", is also used in wrapped sushi. The scallop in the photograph is from Notsuke in Hokkaido Prefecture.

夏
Summer

1月 JAN

3月 MAR

5月 MAY

7月 JUL

9月 SEP

11月 NOV

◈ 江戸前寿司に使う醤油

　江戸初期は上方から高値で買っていたが、文化文政（1804〜30年）頃から、常陸、下総、上総など江戸近郊で盛んに作られるようになり、江戸の人々の好みに合わせて質のいい濃口醤油（→P.154）が登場してからは、江戸の醤油は関東物で占められるようになる。

　現代と違って、江戸前では醤油をそのまま握りに使う習慣はなく、たいていの握りは「煮切り」（→P.154）をさっと塗って出された。他にはツメ（→P.154）を塗ったりヅケ（→P.154）にするなど、食べる側が自分で醤油をつけることはなかったのである。

◈ The soy sauce used in *Edomae-zushi*

In the early part of the Edo Period it was purchased from Kansai region at great expense, but during the Bunka Bunsei Era (1804 to 1830) production of soy sauce became widespread in the areas around Edo which are now Chiba and Ibaraki Prefecture. Once this dark and high quality soy sauce, which suited the tastes of Edo citizens, arrived, it completely dominated the market for soy sauce in the city. It would be fair to say that it was this encounter with soy sauce that led to the advent of *Edomae-zushi*.

Unlike nowadays, soy sauce was not used as it stood in Edomae sushi, but was turned into a sauce called *nikiri*[1] that was brushed on the sushi before serving. A salty-sweet sauce (*tsume*[2]) was sometimes applied to the sushi, or it may have been soaked in soy sauce using the *zuke*[3] method. The customers themselves would not, however, have applied the soy sauce.

 *1-3 Please see page 154

その他

Others

穴子

あなご

ANAGO
Sea eel

　穴子は夏の江戸前の代表的な寿司ネタ。長さ1mほどのものが脂の乗りが最高の状態で、醤油や酒の煮汁で煮ると、皮の表面に脂が浮かび上がってくる。穴子には多くの種類があるが、寿司では全国各地で底引き網で獲れる真穴子が握られる。

　写真のように1貫の炙って焼いた穴子を半分に切って、塩、ツメ（→P.154）を施し、2種類を供する店もある。塩を振ったほうには柚の香を効かせると、穴子そのものの甘さが引き立って、実にすがすがしい。どちらも、口に入れた途端にはらっとほぐれて溶けていき、食感はあくまでやさしい。

　写真の穴子は長崎・対馬産。

Sea eel is one of the representative ingredients of *Edomae-zushi* in the summer. Sea eels that have reached a length of around one meter have the best amount of fat on them, and this fat appears on the surface of their skin when simmered together with soy sauce and sake. There are many varieties of sea eel, but it is the *maanago* or white-spotted eel, caught all around Japan with dragnets, that is used in sushi.

As can be seen in the photograph, the eel is toasted, sliced in half, salted or brushed with the *tsume*[1], sometimes being served in both varieties. When the salted type is flavored with the aroma of the *yuzu* citrus fruit it brings out the sweetness of the sea eel, and is most refreshing. However it is served, as soon as you eat the sea eel it dissolves and melts in your mouth with a texture that is always gentle.

The sea eel in the photograph is from Tsushima in Nagasaki Prefecture.

1月 JAN

3月 MAR

5月 MAY

7月 JUL

9月 SEP

11月 NOV

　　*1-3 Please see page 154

FISH FACT

- 学名／Scientific name：
  Conger myriaster

- 主産地／Most caught in：
  愛知、兵庫、島根、長崎、宮城など／
  AICHI, HYOGO, SHIMANE, NAGASAKI, MIYAGI, etc.

- 地方名／Local names：
  ホンアナゴ、ハカリメ、メジロ、ベラタなど／
  HONANAGO, HAKARIME, MEJIRO, BERATA, etc.

- 分布／Distribution：
  日本各地、東シナ海／Around Japan, East China Sea

海胆 <ruby>うに</ruby>

UNI
Sea urchin

　日本近海に生息する180種類ほどの海胆のうち、食用にされるのは10種類前後で、なかでも最高峰の海胆が馬糞海胆である。殻はやや扁平な饅頭型。直径約4cmと小ぶりで、短い棘が密生する。

　海胆は、雌雄を問わず、生殖巣を食用とするが、寿司屋で握られるのは、鮮やかなオレンジ色をした卵巣の部分のみ。

　海胆は食べる餌によって味が変わり、北海道のおいしい高級昆布を食べて育った馬糞海胆の味は絶品だ。

　濃厚な甘みと香りが口いっぱいに広がっていく。

　写真の馬糞海胆は北海道・浜中産。

Of the approximately 180 varieties of sea urchin which exist in Japanese coastal waters, about 10 varieties are edible, with *bafun uni* (sea urchins) thought to be the best. Sea urchins are flattish and similar to a bun in shape. With a diameter of roughly 4 centimetres, they are rather small and covered in short spines.

The gonads of both male and female sea urchins can be eaten but only the bright orange-colored roe are used for *nigiri-zushi*.

The flavor of sea urchin varies according to what they feed on and the flavor of the sea urchins that have been nourished on the delicious, top quality kelp of Hokkaido is exquisite.

A heavy sweetness and aroma of the sea urchins spreads throughout the mouth when eaten.

The sea urchins shown in the photograph are from Hamana-ka in Hokkaido Prefecture.

春〜夏
From spring to summer

1月 JAN

3月 MAR

5月 MAY

7月 JUL

9月 SEP

11月 NOV

今では全国で食べられているウニの軍艦巻きは、1941年頃に初代の今田壽治（ひさじ）氏がお客の注文を受けて考案したのがはじまり。当時は第二次世界大戦が始まっており、そうした時代背景から、業界の人が「軍艦巻き」と名付けたという。

The sea urchin *gunkanmaki* now eaten all over the country was first created in 1941 by Hisaji Imada, who came up with the idea based on a customer's order. Against a backdrop of the Second World War, it gained the name "Battleship roll".

FISH FACT

● 学名／ Scientific name：

Hemicentrotus pulcherrimus

● 主産地／ Most caught in：

北海道、青森、岩手、宮城／

HOKKAIDO, AOMORI, IWATE, MIYAGI

● 地方名／ Local names：

がぜ、がんぜ、あか／ GAZE, GANZE, AKA

● 分布／ Distribution：

朝鮮半島〜択捉島／

From the Korean Peninsula to the Etorofu

イクラ <ruby>いくら</ruby>

IKURA
Salmon roe

イクラはロシア語で魚卵全般のことを指している。

日本では白鮭の魚卵が使われるのがほとんどで、たいていは産地で加工される。9月から10月のやや早い時期のイクラは皮膜が薄いため、口に入れたときのなめらかさが格段に違う。

この時期の卵を一つひとつばらし、醤油や酒などで作った漬け汁に入れて寝かせると、うまみが一粒一粒に入り込み、寿司ネタの生イクラとして生まれ変わる。

イクラは軍艦で握る。最後に柚をひと振りすると、イクラの粒からほとばしるうまみに柚が香り、海苔がアクセントとなって味を引き締めてくれる。

写真のイクラは岩手・普代産。

Ikura derives from the Russian word for fish eggs.

Most of the salmon roe used in Japan comes from chum salmon and are usually processed at its place of origin. Salmon roe that is harvested fairly early in the season, in either September to October, have a thin membrane and a unique, smooth texture.

Roe harvested at this time are separated gently and then marinated in a mixture of soy sauce, sake, etc., to be transformed into a topping for sushi.

Ikura are made into *gunkan-maki*. Finished off with a squeeze of yuzu, or Japanese citrus fruit, the umami of the salmon roe combines with the fragrance of the *yuzu* citrus, with the nori providing an additional accent to draw all the flavors together.

The salmon roe shown in the photograph are from Fudai in Iwate Prefecture.

秋 Fall

1月 JAN
3月 MAR
5月 MAY
7月 JUL
9月 SEP
11月 NOV

FISH FACT

● 学名／Scientific name：

Oncorhynchus keta

● 主産地／Most caught in：

北海道、岩手、宮城、青森、秋田、富山など／

HOKKAIDO, IWATE, MIYAGI, AKITA, TOYAMA, etc.

● 地方名／Local names：

アキザケ、シロザケ、シャケなど／AKIZAKE, SHIROZAKE, SHAKE, etc.

● 分布／Distribution：

千葉県利根川、日本海山口県以北、北太平洋／ North of Tone river(CHIBA),

Sea of Japan north of YAMAGUCHI, The North Pacific

※旬カレンダー含め、データはすべてサケ／
Including the seasonal calendar, all the information refers to salmon

玉子

たまご

TAMAGO
Egg

玉子はそれぞれの寿司屋の特徴が出やすいとされるネ
タで、店の違いは、魚よりもむしろ玉子で分かるともい
える。

江戸前寿司の玉子は、芝海老のすり身を加え、じっく
り焼き上げている。ふんわりとしていながらややこって
りとしたカステラのような風合いで、味わいも奥深い。
この玉子を厚く切って写真のように鞍掛けに握り、1貫
を半分に切って提供される。

芝海老入りの玉子は、握りだけでなく、太巻きやちら
し寿司などにも使われる。

なかにはだし巻き玉子を握る店もあり、こちらはつ
るっとした食感で鰹だしのうまみを包み込んでいる。

You can judge a sushi restaurant by the quality of its omelette.

The egg topping of *Edomae-zushi* includes ground *shiba*
shrimp and is cooked rather slowly. Although light in texture,
this egg topping is quite rich, almost resembling a sponge
cake. As shown in the photograph, this egg topping is cut quite
thickly and presented *kurakake* (saddle) style with one piece cut
in half.

This egg topping made with ground *shiba* shrimp is used in
futomaki and *chirashi-zushi* as well as *nigiri-zushi*.

Some sushi restaurants also make *nigiri-zushi* using rolled
egg omelette with stock from dried bonito and is very smooth-
textured.

1月 JAN

3月 MAR

5月 MAY

7月 JUL

9月 SEP

11月 NOV

玉
ぎょく
GYOKU

D A T A

「銀座 久兵衛」の玉子焼き材料／

Ingredient of the omelette in Ginza Kyubey

● 玉子／ Egg

● 芝海老のすり身／ Minced *shiba* shrimp

● 砂糖、塩、みりん、昆布出汁、少量の醤油など／

　Sugar, Salt, Mirin (type of sweet rice wine used in cooking), seaweed soup, a
　bit of soy sauce

数の子

かずのこ

KAZUNOKO
Herring roe

数の子は、鰊（にしん）の卵を加工したもの。
　一度天日（てんぴ）で干した数の子は、その間にうまみがぐっと凝縮される。
　その干し数の子を1週間ほどかけて戻して使う。干し数の子は食塩水を朝晩1回ずつ取り替え、漬け汁に漬け込むという手間をかけている。それだけに、ほとんどの店ではなかなかお目にかかれない、実に貴重な寿司ネタとなっている。
　寿司に握ったときの歯ごたえは爽快極まりなく、一粒一粒の弾け具合は、まさに別格である。
　黄金色に輝く写真の数の子は米アラスカ州シトカ産。築地市場でも、干し数の子のせりは年に1回限りだという。

Kazunoko refers to the processed roe from herring.

The roe have been dried in the sun and during this time the taste becomes even more con densed.

The dried herring roe are first rehydrated over a one-week period during which time it are soaked in salted fresh water which is changed each morning and night, then pickled. Kazunoko require a lot of time and effort, so,many sushi restaurants don't use it, making it quite an unusual topping.

The texture as a sushi topping is extremely pleasant, with the superb sensation of feeling each egg pop inside one's mouth.

The golden-colored herring roe in the photograph are from Sitka, Alaska. Even at Tsukiji, Japan's biggest and most famous fish market, the auction for dried herring roe is only held once a year.

1月 JAN

3月 MAR

5月 MAY

7月 JUL

9月 SEP

11月 NOV

● 学名／ Scientific name：

Clupea pallasii

● 主産地／ Most caught in：

北海道／ HOKKAIDO

● 地方名／ Local names：

カド、カドワシ、ハナジロ、ハナグロ／

KADO, KADOWASHI, HANAJIRO, HANAGURO

● 分布／ Distribution：

犬吠埼以北、日本海、渤海〜カリフォルニア半島／

North of INUBOUSAKI, Japan Sea, from Bohai sea to Baja California

※データはすべてニシン／ All the information refers to herrings

太巻き

ふとまき

FUTOMAKI
Thick roll

　寿司屋の個性が発揮される太巻き。太巻きはおみやげとして人気の高い一品だろう。

　写真の太巻きの主役の具は「焼き穴子」と、芝海老のすり身の入った「玉子」の2つ。これに、甘辛く煮た椎茸と干瓢、キュウリ、茹でて車海老などが脇を固めている。江戸前の伝統的な仕事が施された厳選素材を、コシヒカリのシャリとともに、ぱりっと炙った焼き海苔で一気に巻き上げる。

　ひと口にほおばれば、まず焼き穴子の香ばしさが広がり、ふくよかな玉子の存在を感じたかと思うと、突然圧倒的な口福が訪れる。重量感のわりに、2切れ3切れは楽にいけてしまうから何とも驚きだ。

A sushi restaurant can show its individuality through its *futomaki*, which is a popular take-out item.

The main ingredients in the *futomaki* shown in the photograph are grilled conger eel and egg omelette with ground *shiba* shrimps in it. Other ingredients include shiitake mushrooms and *kanpyo* (dried gourd strips) boiled with sugar and soy sauce, cucumber and boiled *kuruma* shrimp (Japanese tiger prawn). The carefully selected ingredients, processed according to *edomae* traditions, are wrapped up together with cooked *koshihikari* brand sushi rice, the most expensive type available with crisp toasted nori, in one smooth movement.

If one piece is eaten in a single mouthful, first you will taste the fragrant grilled conger eel followed by the fluffy egg omelette, which is a very pleasurable experience. Although it may appear heavy, you will be surprised at how easy it is to consume 2-3 pieces.

1月 JAN

3月 MAR

5月 MAY

7月 JUL

9月 SEP

11月 NOV

D A T A

「銀座 久兵衛」太巻きの具材／FUTOMAKI filling in Ginza Kyubey

● 干瓢 KANPYO ／ Dried gourd strips

● キュウリ KYURI ／ Cucumber

● 椎茸 SHIITAKE ／ Shiitake mushroom

● 穴子 ANAGO ／ Conger

● 海老 EBI ／ *kuruma* shrimp(Japanese tiger prawn)

● 玉子 TAMAGO ／ Egg omelette with ground *shiba* shrimps

干瓢巻き

かんぴょうまき
KANPYOMAKI
Gourd strip roll

通年
All season

1月 JAN

3月 MAR

5月 MAY

7月 JUL

9月 SEP

11月 NOV

　江戸前の寿司屋で単に海苔巻きと言えば、干瓢巻きを指す　干瓢は夕顔の実をひも状に剥いて干したもので、発祥の地名から「木津巻き」とも呼ぶ。

　7月中旬から8月中旬に加工された干瓢が色も白く、厚みもあって煮崩れしない最高級品になるようである。

　仕入れた干瓢は、水洗いと塩揉みをして戻し、水煮してから醤油と砂糖で煮る。やわらかいながらも絶妙な歯ごたえが楽しめ、安心感にひたれる巻き物である。

At an *Edomae-zushi* restaurant, *nori-maki* simply refers to *kanpyo-maki* (gourd strip roll). *Kanpyo* is the fruit of the white-flowered gourd that has been shaved into long strips and dried. *Kanpyo-maki* is also called *Kizumaki* after its place of origin.

The highest quality *kanpyo* is that processed from mid-July to mid-August, is white in color, thick and will not fall apart when boiled.

After being washed and then rubbed with salt, the *kanpyo* strips are first boiled in water and then cooked again in soy sauce and sugar. Although the finished product is soft, the *kanpyo* still retains its characteristic texture and is a reliable standby for rolled sushi.

鉄火巻き

<ruby>鉄火巻き<rt>てっかまき</rt></ruby>
TEKKAMAKI
Tuna roll

　<ruby>鉄火<rt>てっか</rt></ruby>巻きの鉄火は真っ赤に熱した鉄のことを意味している。<ruby>鮪<rt>まぐろ</rt></ruby>の赤身を巻いた形が、燃える鉄棒の断面のように見えるところから名づけられたとされる。

　鮪のうまみと海苔の香りが相まって、握りとはまた違った鮪の魅力に出会うことができる。

　干瓢巻きなどとは違い、辛みの効いた山葵を添えて巻かれることが多い。

　赤身で握られることが多いが、大トロや中トロで巻くと、手軽に食べられる鉄火巻きも贅沢な一品となる。

Tekka means a red-hot iron, and this *Tekka-maki*, red flesh tuna, rather resembles a burning iron rod when cut into slices.

The tasty tuna and the fragrant nori go well together and you will encounter an appealing taste different to that of *nigiri-zushi* with tuna.

In contrast to *kanpyo-maki*, these rolls are often prepared with hot wasabi.

Although mostly made with red flesh tuna, when *tekka-maki* is made with *otoro* or *chutoro*, the everyday is transformed into something much more luxurious.

1月 JAN

3月 MAR

5月 MAY

7月 JUL

9月 SEP

11月 NOV

カッパ巻き

かっぱまき
KAPPAMAKI
Cucumber roll

　カッパ巻きは、キュウリを巻いた海苔巻き。キュウリが伝説の河童の大好物というところから、この名がついた。しかし、胡瓜をただ巻くのとはわけが違う。

　写真は味の際立つ「姫キュウリ」を使っている。細く斜め切りし、巻きの幅と調整しながら全体的に均等になるように乗せ、そこに胡麻を振り、一気に巻く。

　心地よい歯ごたえと清涼感。最後に食するのは干瓢巻きか、カッパ巻きにするか、悩ましいところである。

1月 JAN

3月 MAR

5月 MAY

7月 JUL

9月 SEP

11月 NOV

Kappa-maki is a seaweed roll made with cucumber. The name refers to the *kappa*[1], a legendary Japanese water imp who is fond of cucumbers. But it is not just a simple matter of making a roll with cucumber in the middle.

The *kappa-maki* shown in the photograph uses the very tasty cucumber variety called *Hime Kyuuri*. Cut diagonally into thin sticks, the cucumber is carefully laid out on the sushi rice so that the roll will be even throughout. Then, after a sprinkling of sesame seeds, it is all rolled up in one smooth movement.

What a good texture and refreshing effect! Whether to have *kappa-maki* or *kanpyo-maki* at the end of the meal is a difficult choice.

*1 Please see page 154

沢庵巻き

たくあんまき
TAKUANMAKI
Pickled roll

沢庵を刻み、大葉と胡麻とで巻いた巻き物。沢庵とは、大根を糠で漬けた漬け物のこと。

沢庵はそのまま使わず、切手から塩抜きをし、醤油とだしの漬け汁に浸すというひと手間が加わる。シャリの上に細かく刻んだ沢庵、紫蘇を乗せ、胡麻を振って、一瞬で巻く。鮮烈な香りの調和をいただく一品。

ぽりぽりとした食感と、大葉と胡麻の風味豊かな味わいを楽しめるとして人気の細巻きだ。

This roll includes *takuan* or *daikon* radish pickled in a fermented medium of rice bran and brine, as well as *shiso* leaf and sesame seeds.

Takuan must first be desalted and is then left to steep in a combination of soy sauce and stock. *Takuan* thus prepared is then cut into appropriate sizes and laid upon the sushi rice. After topping with shiso and sprinkled sesame seeds, it is all rolled up in one smooth movement. The harmony of strong flavors is striking.

Takuan-maki is a popular *hoso-maki* (thin roll) because of its crunchy texture and the rich aromas of the *shiso* and sesame seeds.

通年
All season

1月 JAN

3月 MAR

5月 MAY

7月 JUL

9月 SEP

11月 NOV

ちらし寿司

ちらしずし

CHIRASHIZUSHI
Assorted sashimi on rice

　寿司飯の上にさまざまな具を散らしていくところから、ちらし寿司の名がついた。バラちらし、単にちらしともいう。具を乗せていく方法と、混ぜ込む方法があり、店によって仕上がりの印象は大きく異なってくる。

　写真のバラちらしは、まず酢飯を作る際に、戻して煮た干し椎茸、ガリを混ぜ込んでおく。飾りつけの材料は季節によって変動するが、斜め切りした穴子の蒲焼き、芝海老のすり身入りの玉子、薄切りにした筍、茹でた車海老、絹さや（さやえんどう）、刻み海苔などである。

　写真の　品はこのバラちらしに刺身の盛り合わせがついたもの。バラちらしに乗せて食べるのもよし、刺身として味わうのもよし、という豪華な一品だ。

Literally "scattered sushi", this dish may also be called *bara-chirashi* or simply *chirashi*. Ingredients may just be scattered on top or they may be mixed in with the rice, so depending on the sushi restaurant, the end result may look entirely different.

In the *bara-chirashi* shown in the photograph, dried shiitake mushrooms that were rehydrated and cooked have been mixed in with the rice together with *gari* (pickled ginger). The toppings vary according to the season, but may include diagonally-cut pieces of braised conger eel, egg omelette with ground *shiba* shrimps mixed in, thinly sliced bamboo shoots, boiled shrimps, snow peas and shredded nori.

One item shown in the photograph is *bara-chirashi* with sashimi served on another plate. The sashimi in this lavish dish could be eaten together with the rice or enjoyed simply as sashimi.

1月 JAN

3月 MAR

5月 MAY

7月 JUL

9月 SEP

11月 NOV

生ちらし

なまちらし
NAMACHIRASHI

「銀座 久兵衛」ではちらし寿司のことは「生ちらし」、刺身がついていないおみやげ用のものを「バラちらし」と呼ぶ
At the Ginza Kyubey sushi restaurant, *chirashi-zushi* is called *nama-chirashi*, while *chirashi-zushi* specifically for taking out is called *barachirashi* and does not include any sashimi.

海外で人気の寿司ネタ
Sushi toppings popular outside of Japan

　海外では、海苔を使わないロール寿司からSUSHI人気に火がついた。生の魚介類の代わりにアボカドやマンゴーなど、日本の寿司では考えられない食材が寿司ネタとして好まれている。その後これらは日本に逆輸入され、回転寿司などで出されている。

　海苔を使う場合は、酢飯の内側に巻き込んで「裏巻き」にすることが多い。裏巻きとは、外側が酢飯、内側に海苔という巻き方で、通常の巻き寿司とは逆になる。巻き方は、海苔の上に酢飯を乗せ、ラップをかけてひっくり返し、返した海苔の上に具を置いてラップを巻き簀のように巻いていく。

　カリフォルニアロールやサーモンとアボカドロールで酢飯と海苔に親しんだ後は、外国人客も日本の伝統的な江戸前寿司に挑戦していただきたい。

Outside of Japan, sushi roll that doesn't use nori at all sparked a sushi boom. Ingredients such as avocado and mango are preferred in place of raw seafood, something that is unthinkable of with traditional Japanese sushi. These ideas have subsequently been reimported back into Japan and appear at *kaiten-zushi* (conveyor belt sushi) bars and so on.

When nori is used, it is often used on the inside with rice on the outside, to make *ura-maki* (inside-out roll). With ura-maki, the sushi rice is on the outside and nori is on the inside, the complete opposite of an ordinary *nori-maki*. To make this type of roll, the sushi rice is placed on top of the sheet of nori and turned upside down after having been covered with cling-wrap. The other ingredients are placed directly on top of the sheet of nori and the cling-wrap is used to roll it up in place of the usual bamboo mat.

After you have gotten used to sushi with California rolls and salmon and avocado rolls, we hope that you will also try Japanese traditional *Edomae-zushi*.

* P.132-133 PHOTO BY "SHARI THE TOKYO SUSHI BAR"

カリフォルニアロール

California roll

カニ風味蒲鉾、アボカドを具にマヨネーズで和え、裏巻きにする。

An inside-out roll made with crab sticks and avocado, dressed with mayonnaise.

サーモンとアボカドロール

Salmon and Avocado roll

外国人はサーモンの寿司が大好き。アボカドとの相性も抜群。

Non-Japanese are very fond of salmon sushi. Salmon and avocado go very well together.

マンゴーロール

Mango roll

好きな具をシャリと海苔で巻き、色鮮やかなマンゴーを乗せる。

Make a roll using ingredients you like together with the sushi rice and nori and finish it with colourful pieces of mango.

上記のロール寿司が食べられる店／A restaurant where you can try the sushi rolls above

**SHARI
THE TOKYO
SUSHI BAR**

●シャリザトウキョウスシバー

住所：東京都中央区銀座2-4-18
アルボーレ銀座ビル8F
電話：03-5524-8788
営業時間：11:30〜15:00、17:30〜23:30
（木・金曜は17:30〜24:00）
定休日：第3月曜・日曜のディナー
Address: ALBORE GINZA 8F
Ginza 2-4-18, Chuo-ku, Tokyo
Telephone: 03-5524-8788
Hours: 11:30-15:00, 17:30-23:30
(Thu & Fri 17:30-24:00)
Open everyday except Sunday evening and the third Monday of the month

◆ 魚の旬

　魚の旬とは、一般的に身が充実し、脂が乗り、うまさを最大限に発揮する時季である。しかし、実際のとらえ方は多様で、「走り」「盛り」「名残」があるとされる。

　季節を先取りし、うまさは未熟ながらも出始めのものを珍重して食すものを「走り」という。魚の旬は一般に産卵期前といわれ、産卵前の活発に餌を食べて脂の乗ったものはうまさの「盛り」となる。産卵直前は海面や浅瀬に集まってくるため漁獲量が増えるが、すでにうまさのピークを過ぎていることが多く、「名残」を惜しむ時期に差しかかる。

　南北に長い日本列島は産卵期にかなり幅がある。地域や文化の違い、個人的嗜好からも旬を一概に決めるのは難しい。

◆ The best season for each fish

When fish are in season, the flesh is generally firm with a high fat content and is most delicious then. However, "season" can actually be split into different periods such as *hashiri* (early season), *sakari* (peak season) and *nagori* (late season).

Hashiri refers to when fish have just started to come on the market and are highly sought after even though they are still not mature in flavor. *sakari* (peak season) is before the fish spawn and they feed actively, acquiring a high fat content. Just before spawning, shoals of fish gather on the ocean's surface or in the shallows and thus catches increase. However, by this time, the fish have already passed their peak condition, which Japanese people start to miss in this *nagori* (late) season.

The Japanese archipelago stretches north to south over a long distance. Deciding exactly when peak season is can be difficult due to differences in localities, culture and individual tastes.

寿司屋の料理

Dish of the sushi restaurant

お通し とお *OTOSHI* / Appetizer served as soon as a customer sits down

注文した品とは別に、最初に小鉢などで提供される一品料理。写真は「大根とワカメのサラダ」。

Otoshi is an appetizer usually served in a small dish, separate to anything the customer has ordered. The photograph shows a salad of *daikon* radish and *wakame* seaweed.

珍味 ちん み *CHINMI* / delicacies

白子 しら こ *SHIRAKO* / Soft roe

鱈、鮟鱇、河豚など魚類の精巣をボイルする。酢の物が多い。

Shirako is the boiled sperm sack of fish such as cod, monkfish or blowfish (fugu), which is often served with vinegar.

あん肝 きも *ANKIMO* / Monkfish liver

ボイルした鮟鱇の肝臓。ポン酢と紅葉おろしでいただく。

Ankimo is the liver of monkfish which is boiled and then served with *ponzu* and *momijioroshi* (*daikon* and chili grated together).

イクラ *IKURA* / Salmon roe

鮭の卵の醤油漬け・塩漬け。鮭の切り身と和えたりもする。

Ikura (salmon roe), are marinated in soy sauce or pickled in salt. Sometimes they are eaten mixed together with pieces of salmon.

刺身 SASHIMI / Sliced raw fish

　旬の魚を仕入れる寿司屋ならではの新鮮な刺身。盛り合わせで楽しみたい。一般的に山葵や生姜などの薬味が添えられる。

　Sashimi, or slices of raw fish, are very fresh, as only a sushi restaurant could get straight from a fish market. Enjoying a selection of sashimi is preferable. Sashimi is usually accompanied by garnishes such as wasabi or ginger.

焼き物 YAKIMONO / Grilled Dishes

　焼き魚も人気。写真は赤鯥の焼き魚。刺身にする魚を惜しげもなく焼く。コースメニューに含まれていることが多い。

　Yakimono, or grilled fish, is also popular. Shown in the photograph is akamutsu (blackthroat seaperch). Fish that could have been used for sashimi are quite often grilled instead and included in set courses.

茶碗蒸し CHAWAN-MUSHI / Savory steamed egg custard with assorted ingredients

茶碗蒸しは寿司屋の定番的一品。写真の茶碗蒸しには百合根、芝海老、かまぼこ、三つ葉が入り、餡がかけられている。

Chawan-mushi, savory steamed egg custard, is a standard item at sushi restaurants. The egg custard in the photograph contains lily root, *shiba* shrimp, boiled fish-paste, and a Japanese herb *mitsuba*, and is topped off with a thick sauce.

味噌汁 MISOSHIRU / Miso soup

写真は蜆の味噌汁。味噌汁も店や季節によってさまざまな具材の味噌汁が楽しめる。寿司屋ではだしを取るのに、大きな魚のアラや蟹が大胆に使われることも多い。

Shown in the photograph is *miso-shiru* (miso soup), with corbicula clams. Many different kinds of miso soup can be enjoyed, depending on the restaurant and the various ingredients according to the seasons. Sushi restaurants usually make clever use of the leftover parts of fish and crab for making soup stock.

寿司に合う酒 Sake to suit sushi

　寿司の邪魔をせず、寿司の味を引き立てる酒。しかし、重要なのは、魚の種類よりも醤油との相性。寿司に酒を合わせる場合、味ももちろんだが、酒の香りが関係してくる。

　日本酒なら基本的に純米か本醸造を選ぶ。火を通したネタには燗、生がうまいネタには冷酒と、温度を意識してもよい。吟醸など香り重視の繊細な酒は合わないとされる。

　ワインならスパークリングかソーヴィニョン・ブランなど。酒と一緒にお茶も出してもらうことをおすすめしたい。

Sake should not interfere with the taste of sushi; instead, it should draw out the flavors. However, what is important is the compatibility with soy sauce rather than with the various types of fish. As well as the taste, the aroma of the sake is also important when deciding which kind would suit sushi.

You should choose either *junmai* or *honjouzo* types of sake. It is acceptable to show awareness of temperatures by warming up sake to go with dishes that have been cooked and serving sake cold for uncooked dishes. Types of sake such as *ginjo*, with a pronounced aroma and delicate taste, do not really go with sushi.

With wine, choose either a sparkling wine or something like a sauvignon blanc. It is recommend that green tea is served together with alcoholic drinks.

熱燗
ATSUKAN / Hot sake

　寿司には最初から無条件で熱燗という向きもある。燗上がりする純米か本醸造を選びたい。

Some say that *atsukan* (hot sake) is always a good match for sushi. Choose either a *junmai* or *honjouzo* that taste even better after having been heated up.

◈ 回転寿司

　客席前に設置したチェーンコンベア上に、小皿に載せた寿司を載せて巡らせる形式の安価な寿司店。ほぼセルフサービスに近い店舗形態で、客は好みの寿司を皿ごと取り上げて食べる。価格は皿の色で何段階かに決まっているが、100円均一などを売りにしている大手回転寿司チェーンもある。タッチパネルなどで別途注文することもできる。

　メニューは寿司だけでなく、丼物やデザートもコンベアに乗りぐるぐると回転していく姿は、初めて回転寿司を体験する人にとって不思議な光景であるようだ。

　昨今の寿司ブームにより、海外にも回転寿司屋が多く見られるようになった。

◈ *Kaiten-zushl*

Kaiten-zushi is a cheap sushi restaurant where plates carrying sushi travel past customers via a conveyor belt It is more or less self-service,with customers choosing the plates of sushi they want to eat.Various levels of price are represented in the different colors for the plates although some large *kaiten-zushi* restaurants charge only 100 yen per plate.

It may also be possible to place orders separately using a touchscreen. Other dishes may be on the menu such as *don-mono* (a rice bowl with some kind of topping) and desserts. The sight of these rotating on a conveyor belt may appear to be a curious sight for people.

Due to the recent sushi boom, it is now possible to see many *kaiten-zushi* restaurants overseas too.

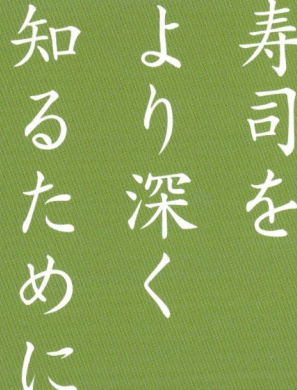

寿司を
より深く
知るために

Chapter 3

Getting to know sushi
more deeply

寿司屋での振る舞い
Sushi etiquette

寿司屋にはフランス料理のようなかしこまったマナーなどはないが、大声で話したり、きつい香水など他の人の迷惑になることは避けたい。調理人と向かい合うスタイルだけに、出された寿司はなるべく早く食べることも意外と大事なポイントだ。

Customers in sushi restaurants don't have to abide by formal etiquette rules for dining such as that for French cuisine but it is better to avoid talking in loud voices, wearing strong perfume and so on. As the chef is positioned very close to customers, when sushi is put in front of you, eating it promptly is actually quite an important point.

Step 1　事前予約 Making a reservation in advance

初めての寿司屋は入りづらいもの。そんなときは電話予約を入れ、予算を提示して料理内容を確認するとよい。

Trying a sushi restaurant for the first time can be difficult. Making a reservation in advance by phone enables you to tell them your budget and get an idea of the content beforehand.

Step 2　どこに座るのがいい？ Where to sit?

せっかくの寿司屋。テーブル席では、寿司屋の楽しみの半分しか得られない。職人との会話を楽しみ、職人の手仕事とさまざまなネタを見ながら食べられるカウンター席に座るのがベストである。

Having made the effort to come to the sushi restaurant, deciding to sit at a table will cut your enjoyment by half. Sitting up at the counter is best for exchanging polite banter with the chef while observing them carrying out their work and enables you to see the various kinds of sushi ingredients while you eat.

メニュー選び Choosing what to eat

　寿司の注文パターンは大ざっぱに言って「おまかせ」「お好み」「お決まり」の3種類。

　「おまかせ」はネタの選択を寿司職人に任せ、その日のおすすめのネタを握ってもらうこと。予約時に予算を伝えておけば安心できる。「お好み」は食べたいネタを自分のペースで選んで注文すること。「お決まり」は価格と内容が設定されており、「松」「竹」「梅」などのセットになっている。

Methods of ordering in a sushi restaurant can roughly be divided into three types: *omakase* (leaving it up to the chef), *okonomi* (a la carte), and *okimari* (a set course).

Omakase means that you leave the choice of sushi toppings up to the chef and get them to make sushi according to what they recommend for that day. If you let the restaurant know your budget beforehand, when making the reservation, you won't have to worry about the bill being too expensive. *Okonomi* means that you order what you want to eat at your own pace. *Okimari* means eating some set course such as *sho* (pine), *chiku* (bamboo), and *bai* (plum) which represent the priciest, mid-range, and least expensive set courses.

寿司を食べる順番
The order in which to eat sushi

　寿司を食べる順番には決まりがあると思われがちだが、実際には
そのようなものはない。好きな順番で注文できるのが寿司のいいと
ころである。

「おまかせ」で出される一例として、中トロ→白身→貝類→光り物
→煮物→巻物→玉子という順番があるが、あくまでも選択肢のひと
つに過ぎない。店によって、白身や貝類など繊細な味のものから始
め、味の濃いものにしていくというところもあるが、これも順番に
決まりがないことを表している。

It is widely thought that a set order exists for eating sushi but
actually there is no such thing. Being able to order what you
want when you want to is the good thing about eating at a sushi
restaurant.

To give an example of what would be provided for *Omakase*:
chutoro; white flesh fish; some kind of shellfish; fish such as
mackerel or sardines with a silver sheen; *nimono* (fish boiled in
stock with salty-sweet flavor); *makimono* (rolled sushi), egg omelette. This is just one example of what may be given to customers. Depending on the restaurant, it may begin with white flesh
fish or shellfish with delicate flavors moving gradually to items
with stronger flavors. This simply shows that there is no rule on
the order to be followed.

例えば… For example

1　**平目**
HIRAME /
Japanese flounder

2　**小鰭**
KOHADA /
Mid-sized *konoshiro*
gizzard shad

3　**中トロ**
CHUTORO /
Tuna

Step 5 　お茶を飲む、ガリを食べるタイミング
When to drink green tea and eat gari (pickled ginger)

　お茶は食後に飲むものと思われている節がある。寿司の世界ではお茶のことを「アガリ」といい、完了やゴールを連想させるが、元は「上がり花」といって、いれ立てのお茶を指す言葉。最初からお茶を頼んで寿司を楽しみたい。

　寿司の脇に盛られた生姜の酢漬けのことを、寿司屋では「ガリ」という。種類の違う寿司を食べるとき、前に食べた寿司の味を消し、口の中をさっぱりさせるために食べる。

There is one school of thought that suggests green tea should be drunk only at the end of the meal. In the world of sushi green tea is known as *agari*, which can mean "end" in Japanese. It is a word that brings to mind the reaching of a goal, but it originally derives from the word *agari-bana*, which was merely an expression used to describe freshly brewed tea. It is quite acceptable for you to order tea before eating, and enjoy it with your sushi throughout the meal.

The slices of ginger that are pickled in vinegar and served as an accompaniment to sushi are called *gari* in sushi restaurants. The purpose of eating this ginger is to cleanse the palate and remove the taste of the piece of sushi you have just eaten, so you can enjoy the flavor of your next piece.

Step 6 　支払いをする When paying your bill

　寿司屋の料金は特に「お好み」を頼むとわかりづらいが、基本的に食べた寿司の種類や量から算出される。酒やつまみを頼めばそれだけ割高になる。カード払いできない店も多い。

The sushi restaurants' bills are hard to understand when ordering *okonomi* (a la carte) but they are basically calculated according to the varieties you have eaten and the amount. Of course, if you have any alcoholic drinks and other side dishes your bill will be more expensive. It is worth noting that many sushi restaurants do not accept credit cards.

寿司の握り方 How sushi is molded

　酢飯は必要な人数分をおひつに移し、人肌の温かさに保って
おく。シャリ同士がつかないよう、手のひらを酢で少し湿らせる。

　シャリを取るときは、つぶさないように右手ですくい、2〜
3回で軽くまとめる。手数が多すぎると米はそれだけ締まって
いってしまう。1貫のシャリの量は人それぞれだが、自分がひ
と口で食べられる理想量は、大きさを変えて握ってもらえば、
感覚的にわかるようになる。

　1貫目が出された後、シャリの量が適当だったかどうかを確
認してくれる店もある。シャリの量も客次第なのだ。

The requisite amount of *shari* or sumeshi (sushi rice) for
the diners is placed in a circular wooden container, and kept
at a temperature roughly equivalent to the human skin. The
chef lightly moistens his palms with vinegar in order to pre-
vent the sushi rice from sticking together.

The chef scoops up the sushi rice with his right hand, taking care not to crush it, and roughly shapes it two or three
times. If this is overdone the rice can become stiff. The size of
one *kan* (piece) of sushi varies
according from chef to chef,
but if you ask the chef to mold
the rice into a size that you
think you will be able to eat in
one mouthful, he will instinc-
tively understand.

After serving the first piece
of sushi, some sushi restaurants
check with customers that the
size of the piece is all right. The
amount of rice is also up to the
customer to decide.

1 シャリをつぶさないように右手（利き手）でさっとすくい、2〜3回で軽くまとめる。こねたりしない。

The chef takes some sushi rice, taking care not to crush it, in his right hand (or left if he is left handed) and roughly molds it two or three times. He does not knead it.

2 左手指の第1関節から付け根の間にネタを取り、親指で軽く押さえる。手のひらはゆるやかなカーブを描く。

He places the topping on the first joint of his fingers of his left hand, and softly presses it down using his thumb, with his palm describing a gentle curve.

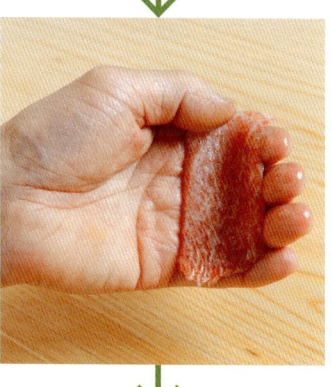

3 右手にシャリを持ったまま、人差し指1本で山葵を取り、左手に乗せたネタの上に山葵をのせる。

Still holding the sushi rice in his right hand, he takes a little wasabi with his index finger and applies it to the topping.

4 ゆるやかなカーブを描いた左手のネタの上に、右手にあったシャリを移し、親指を軽く当てておく。

He then transfers the sushi rice held in his right hand to the topping cradled in his left hand, and lightly presses it with his thumb.

5 シャリの上下をトンと一瞬で押さえて締め、左手の人差し指から小指までを使って、寿司の横側を整える。

He places the rice over the topping and pushes the rice sharply downwards, then neatens the sides of the sushi with all the fingers of his left hand.

6 右手人差し指と中指で上と両端からやわらかく押さえる。一呼吸、二呼吸でネタと合体させる。

He then gently presses the top and both ends with all fingers except his thumb. After a short pause the sushi topping is integrated.

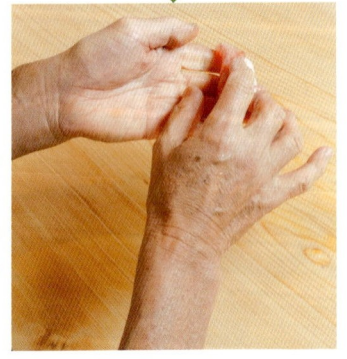

7 目にも止まらぬ速さで、握った寿司をくるっと転がすようにひっくり返し、ネタを上向きにする。

With a speed barely perceptible to the eye, he twists over the molded sushi so the topping side is facing upwards.

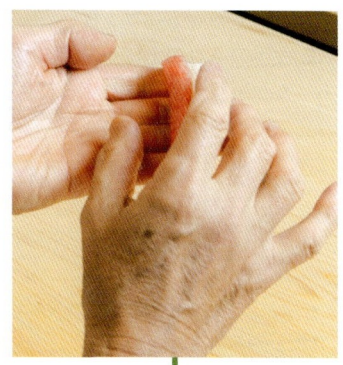

8 この手返しを「小手返し」といい、現在の寿司の主流の握り方となっている。

This flick of the wrist, known as *kotegaeshi*, is the mainstream way of molding sushi nowadays.

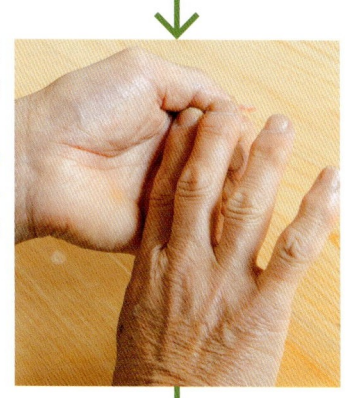

9 全体をやさしく整えたらできあがり。シャリをすくってから握り終わるまで、わずか数秒の早技だ。

When the whole piece has been neatly arranged it is now ready to serve. This lightning-fast movement only a few seconds.

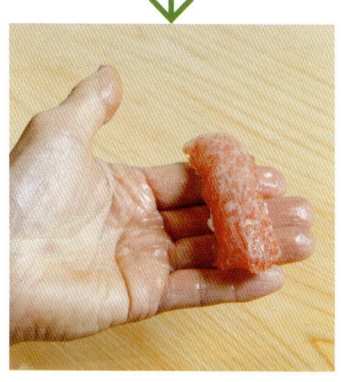

軍艦巻きの握り方 How *gunkanmaki* is made

1 シャリをつぶさないようにさっとすくい、2～3回で軽くまとめる。通常の握り方に比べて箱形にし、まな板に置く。

The chef takes some sushi rice, taking care not to crush it, and roughly molds it two or three times. The rice is molded into a more box-like shape than ordinary sushi, and placed on the chef's chopping board.

2 人差し指で山葵（わさび）をシャリの上に置き、シャリの奥に海苔（のり）を立てて手前に巻き込むようにする。海苔は右側が手前。

The chef applies some wasabi to the sushi rice, and wraps toasted seaweed around the edges. The right side of the toasted seaweed is the front.

3 木箱からヘラで海胆を多めにすくい、巻いた海苔の中のシャリの上に乗せて盛りつける。最後に形を整える。

He then scoops up a quantity of sea urchin from the wooden box it is kept in, and arranges it on top of the sushi rice wrapped in seaweed. Finally the shape is trimmed.

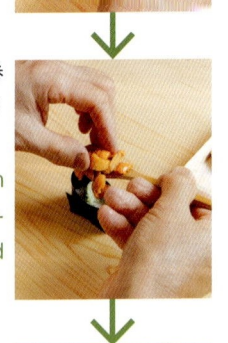

4 海苔の端が浮く場合は2貫目の軍艦で押さえるか、シャリで止める。軍艦巻きのポイントも、手早くやること。

If the seaweed does not stick properly the chef will either attach it with the second piece of *gunkanmaki* or some sushi rice. The point with *gunkanmaki* is to make it quickly.

海苔巻きの巻き方
How *norimaki* (toasted seaweed rolls) are made

❶巻き簀に海苔を置き、❷多めのシャリを取る。❸海苔の中央でシャリを左右に広げ、❹シャリの粒をつぶさないよう指の腹で全体に広げる。❺山葵を乗せ、❻白胡麻を振ってキュウリを乗せ、❼一気に巻いて、❽巻き簀から取り出し、❾半分に切って、さらに3等分する。

❶Toasted seaweed is place on the *makisu* (sushi mat), ❷ A slightly larger amount of sushi rice is taken. ❸The sushi rice is spread out to the left and right from the center of the sushi mat, ❹It is then spread across the whole mat with the underside of the finger, so as not to crush it. ❺Wasabi is applied, ❻White sesame seeds are sprinkled on and cucumber placed on the rice. ❼This is then rolled in one go, ❽ It is removed from the sushi mat, ❾ And then cut into two pieces that are then further cut into thirds.

寿司屋での会話
Conversation at a sushi restaurant

注文 Ordering

「飲み物は何にしますか?」 ➡ 「お茶をお願いします」

Nomimono wa nani ni shimasu ka? ➡ *Ocha o onegai shimasu.*

—What would you like to drink? ➡ I'll have hot green tea.

「メニューを見せてください」

Menu o misete kudasai.

—Please let me take a look at the menu.

「お決まり / お好み / お任せでお願いします」

Okimari/Okonomi/Omakase de onegaishimasu

—I'll have *Okimari* (set menu)/*Okonomi* (a la carte)/*Omakase* (chef's choice).

板前さんとの会話 Conversation with the chef

「食べられない魚はありますか?」 ➡ 「私は海老 / 貝が食べられません」

Taberarenai sakana wa arimasuka?
➡ *Watashi wa ebi/ kai ga taberare masen.*

—Do you have anything fish you can't eat?
➡ I can't eat shrimp/ shellfish.

「生魚が苦手なので、生魚以外の寿司を食べたいです」
➡ 「マグロを炙った握りやエビをボイルした握りができますよ」

Namazakana ga nigate nanode namazakana igai no sushi o tabetai desu.
➡ *Maguro o abutta nigiri ya ebi o boiru shita nigiri ga dekimasuyo.*

—I don't like raw fish, I would like to eat sushi other than raw fish.
➡ You can eat grilled tuna or boiled shrimp.

「山葵は抜いて下さい」

Wasabi wa nuite kudasai.

—Please don't put wasabi into the sushi.

「今日のおすすめは何ですか?」

Kyouno osusume wa nani desuka?

—What is today's recommendation?

「この魚は何ですか?」

Kono sakana wa nani desuka?

—What is this fish?

「醤油に付けて食べるのですか?」

Shoyu o tsukete taberu no desu ka?

—Should I eat this sushi after dipping it in soy sauce?

※握り寿司には味付けされているものと、自分で醤油をつけて食べるものがある。
※ Some kinds of nigirizushi are already seasoned but some should be dipped in soy sauce before eating.

会計時の会話 Conversation at the time of payment

「ごちそうさまでした」

Gochiso sama deshita.

—Thank you for a lovely meal.

「太巻きをおみやげにお願いできますか」

Futomaki o omiyage ni onegai dekimasuka?

—Could I get a fat roll to take out please?

※太巻きをおみやげに販売していない店もあります。
※ Some sushi restaurants don't sell futomaki for take out.

「お勘定をお願いします」

Okanjo o onegai shimasu.

—May I have the check please?

寿司屋用語
Words often used in a sushi restaurant

貫……握り寿司を数える単位
Kan……A unit for counting nigirizushi

ヅケ……魚をダシ醤油につけ込むこと
Zuke……soaked in soy sauce

仕事……江戸前寿司で寿司ネタに手を加えること。魚介を酢で締めたり、茹でたり、煮詰めを塗ったりすること。
Shigoto……This refers to carrying out an extra preparatory step for Edomae sushi toppings, such as boiling, brushing with tsume sauce, or steeping fish in vinegar.

煮切り……みりんや酒を加熱してアルコールを飛ばすこと
Nikiri……boiled down sake or mirin.

ツメ……煮詰めの略。醤油、味醂、酒などを煮詰めんだ塩辛い煮汁のこと。
Tsume……Derives from the words *nizume* (boil down). Soy sauce, mirin, sake and so on are boiled down to make this salty sweet sauce.

酢締め……魚を酢に浸して、身を締めること
Sujime……marinated with vinegar

昆布締め……刺身を昆布で挟み一晩程度置くこと
Kobujime……packed between strips of kelp

濃口醤油……うまみ、甘み、酸味、苦みを併せ持つ代表的な醤油のこと。特に関東地方で醤油というと濃口醤油のことを指す
Koikuchi Shoyu……One of the main types of soy sauce which incorporates umami, sweet, sour and bitter tastes. Especially, in the Kanto region, the words "soy sauce" refer to this kind of soy sauce.

カッパ……日本の妖怪、伝説上の動物。川や沼に住み、きゅうりが好物とされる。
Kappa……One of Japanese goblins, this is a legendary animal which inhabits rivers and lakes and loves cucumbers.

主な日本の産地
Japan's Main Fishing Areas

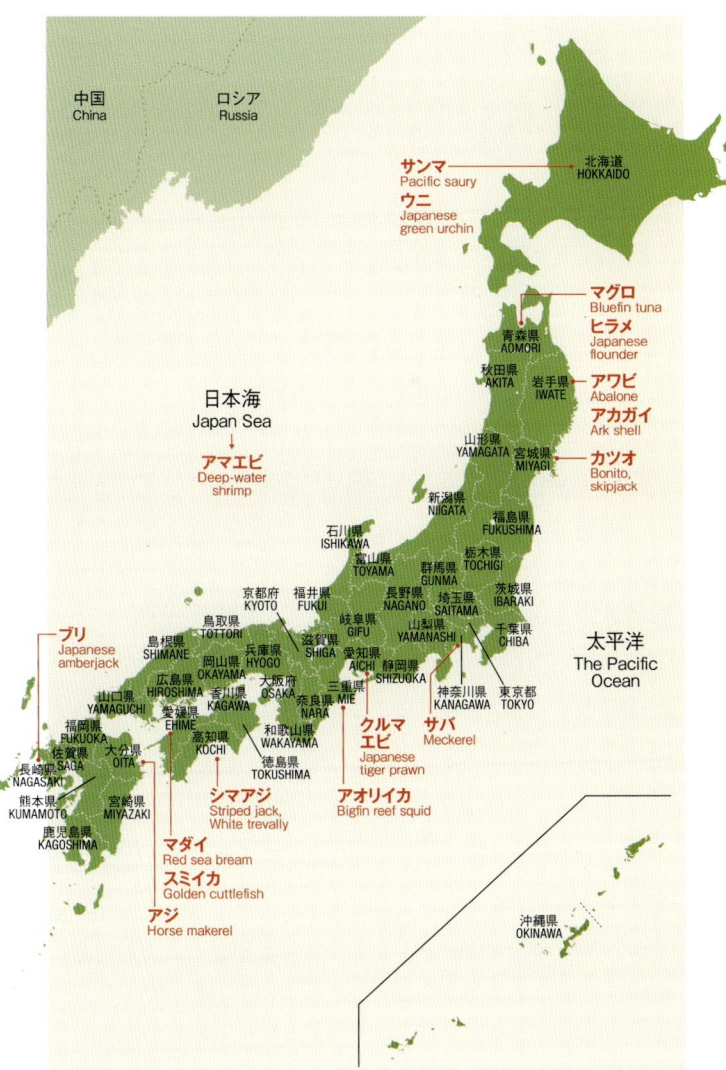

中国
China

ロシア
Russia

サンマ
Pacific saury
ウニ
Japanese
green urchin

北海道
HOKKAIDO

マグロ
Bluefin tuna
ヒラメ
Japanese
flounder

青森県
AOMORI

秋田県
AKITA

岩手県
IWATE

ワビ
Abalone
アカガイ
Ark shell

日本海
Japan Sea

山形県
YAMAGATA

宮城県
MIYAGI

カツオ
Bonito,
skipjack

アマエビ
Deep-water
shrimp

新潟県
NIIGATA

福島県
FUKUSHIMA

石川県
ISHIKAWA

富山県
TOYAMA

栃木県
TOCHIGI

群馬県
GUNMA

茨城県
IBARAKI

京都府
KYOTO

福井県
FUKUI

長野県
NAGANO

埼玉県
SAITAMA

鳥取県
TOTTORI

岐阜県
GIFU

山梨県
YAMANASHI

千葉県
CHIBA

太平洋
The Pacific
Ocean

ブリ
Japanese
amberjack

島根県
SHIMANE

滋賀県
SHIGA

愛知県
AICHI

静岡県
SHIZUOKA

兵庫県
HYOGO

岡山県
OKAYAMA

大阪府
OSAKA

三重県
MIE

神奈川県
KANAGAWA

東京都
TOKYO

山口県
YAMAGUCHI

広島県
HIROSHIMA

香川県
KAGAWA

奈良県
NARA

福岡県
FUKUOKA

愛媛県
EHIME

和歌山県
WAKAYAMA

クルマ
エビ
Japanese
tiger prawn

サバ
Meckerel

佐賀県
SAGA

大分県
OITA

高知県
KOCHI

長崎県
NAGASAKI

徳島県
TOKUSHIMA

熊本県
KUMAMOTO

宮崎県
MIYAZAKI

シマアジ
Striped jack,
White trevally

アオリイカ
Bigfin reef squid

鹿児島県
KAGOSHIMA

マダイ
Red sea bream
スミイカ
Golden cuttlefish

アジ
Horse makerel

沖縄県
OKINAWA

魚	→	英名	1	2	3	4	5	6	7	8	9	10	11	12
鮪 大トロ（まぐろ）	→P.24	Tuna, Bluefin tuna *otoro*	■	■	■							■	■	■
鮪 中トロ（まぐろ）	→P.26	Tuna, Bluefin tuna *chutoro*	■	■	■								■	■
鮪 赤身（まぐろ）	→P.27	Tuna, Bluefin tuna *akami*	■	■	■									
鰹（かつお）	→P.28	Bonito, Skipjack, Oceanic bonito					■	■	■	■	■			
平目（ひらめ）	→P.36	Japanese flounder	■	■	■									
真鯛（まだい）	→P.38	Red sea bream	■	■	■	■								
縞鯵（しまあじ）	→P.40	Striped jack, white trevally							■	■	■			
鰤（ぶり）	→P.42	Japanese amberjack	■	■	■	■								
勘八（かんぱち）	→P.44	Great amberjack							■	■	■			
甘鯛（あまだい）	→P.46	Tilefish	■	■	■									
鱸（すずき）	→P.48	Japanese sea bass						■	■	■				
皮剥（かわはぎ）	→P.50	Threadsail filefish										■	■	■
鱚（きす）	→P.52	Sillago						■	■	■				
鯒（こち）	→P.54	Flathead						■	■	■				
眞子鰈（まこがれい）	→P.55	Marbled flounder	■	■	■	■								
鯵（あじ）	→P.58	Horse mackerel					■	■	■					
鯖（さば）	→P.60	Mackerel	■	■								■	■	■
小鰭（こはだ）	→P.62	Mid-sized konoshiro gizzard shad										■	■	
秋刀魚（さんま）	→P.64	Pacific saury									■	■		
針魚（さより）	→P.66	Japanese halfbeak	■	■	■									
春日子（かすご）	→P.68	Young sea bream			■	■	■							
鰯（いわし）	→P.70	Sardine					■	■	■	■				

※旬の時期はあくまでも目安です。獲れる産地・その年の気候によって旬の時期は前後します。
※The indication about being in season is only a guide. The timing of the season may vary depending on the area where the seafood is harvested and also depending on the weather at that time.

監修・撮影協力

Editorial super visor, Photographic acknowledgments

銀座 久兵衛

TEL：03-3571-6523

住所：東京都中央区銀座8-7-6

営業時間：11:30〜14:00、17:00〜22:00

定休日：日曜、祝日、お盆、年末年始

最寄り駅：東京メトロ銀座線新橋駅3番出口から徒歩5分

　1935年の創業以来、江戸前の味にこだわり、守り続けている名店。美食家としても知られる陶芸家、北大路魯山人や吉田茂元総理など各界の著名人も足繁く通ったことでも有名である。

　名人の呼び声高かった初代、今田壽治氏の技を受け継ぎ、現在は2代目の今田洋輔氏が暖簾を守っている。

　国内の観光客はもちろん、海外からの観光客にも「本場の江戸前寿司を食べられる」と人気だ。

　修行を積んだ職人たちによる江戸前の技と、名店にふさわしい一流のもてなしを楽しめることだろう。

GINZA KYUBEY

Telephone: 03-571-6523

Address: Ginza 8-7-6, Chuo-ku, Tokyo

Hours: 11:30-14:00, 17:00-22:00

Shop holiday: Sunday, Public holiday, Obon around mid-August, End of year and New Year holidays

Nearest station: A 5-minute walk from Exit 3 of Shinbashi Station on the Ginza Line of the Tokyo Metro

A famous sushi restaurant that opened in 1935 and has championed and continued to serve authentic *Edomae-zushi* ever since. It is famed for its well-known clientele, which over the years has included the gourmet and potter Rosanjin Kitaoji, and former Prime Minister Shigeru Yoshida.

The much-talked-about first chef Hisaji Imada passed down his skills to his son, Yosuke Imada. The second-generation chef now preserves the reputation of the restaurant.

It is popular with both tourists from within Japan and overseas, as a place where one can sample "genuine Edomae-zushi".

The *Edomae* skills of craftsmen with an inside-out knowledge of their profession, and the first-class welcome appropriate to a famous restaurant is sure to be enjoyed.

【参考資料】

『銀座久兵衛 こだわりの流儀』(今田洋輔)PHP研究所

『寿司ガイドブック』池田書店

『すし手帳』(坂本一男)東京書籍

『からだにおいしい 魚の便利帳』(藤原昌高)高橋書店

『寿司ネタの通になる』(野村祐三)祥伝社

『Sushi 鮨　バイリンガル版』パイ インターナショナル

撮影協力●銀座 久兵衛 GINZA KYUBEY
編集協力●長谷部祐子(株式会社アーク・コミュニケーションズ)
装丁・本文デザイン・DTP ●石田嘉弘(アズール図案室)
撮影●野田真
執筆●柴山幸夫
イラスト●桜井葉子
翻訳●株式会社バイリンガルグループ
校正●有限会社槍楯社
英文校正●Sophie Knight
魚介写真協力●マルク『生鮮の素.さかなや魚介類図鑑』(ケイザックスコンセプトハウス)
編集担当●齋藤友里(ナツメ出版企画株式会社)

ナツメ社Webサイト
https://www.natsume.co.jp
書籍の最新情報(正誤情報を含む)は
ナツメ社Webサイトをご覧ください。

本書に関するお問い合わせは、書名・発行日・該当ページ
を明記の上、下記のいずれかの方法にてお送りください。
電話でのお問い合わせはお受けしておりません。
・ナツメ社webサイトの問い合わせフォーム
　https://www.natsume.co.jp/contact
・FAX(03-3291-1305)
・郵送(下記、ナツメ出版企画株式会社宛て)
なお、回答までに日にちをいただく場合があります。正誤の
お問い合わせ以外の書籍内容に関する解説・個別の相
談は行っておりません。あらかじめご了承ください。

英語で紹介する 寿司ハンドブック
A SUSHI HANDBOOK IN ENGLISH AND JAPANESE

2013年5月9日　初版発行
2024年5月20日　第10刷発行

監修者　今田洋輔　Imada Yosuke, 2013

発行者　田村正隆

発行所　株式会社ナツメ社
　　　　東京都千代田区神田神保町1-52 ナツメ社ビル1F(〒101-0051)
　　　　電話 03(3291)1257(代表)　FAX 03(3291)5761
　　　　振替 00130-1-58661

制　作　ナツメ出版企画株式会社
　　　　東京都千代田区神田神保町1-52 ナツメ社ビル3F(〒101-0051)
　　　　電話 03(3295)3921(代表)

印刷所　図書印刷株式会社

ISBN978-4-8163-5419-9 Printed in Japan